Information Technology and a New International Order

Jörg Becker

Edited by

**Transnational Data Reporting Service
Amsterdam, The Netherlands**

**Studentlitteratur AB
Chartwell-Bratt Ltd.**

Cover: Kjeld Brandt
© Jörg Becker, 1984
Printed in Sweden
Studentlitteratur
Lund 1984
ISBN 91-44-20611-9 (Studentlitteratur)
ISBN 0-86238-043-X (Chartwell–Bratt)

Contents

Foreword

'It is clear to everyone that the powers conferred by modern science and technology should be available to all, having been brought into being by a whole chain of inventions, spread out in time and space, to which all peoples have contributed and to which they all, therefore, have an equal right of access.

'I have found that – for all of us – advances in modern technology have vastly increased the impact of communication, making it one of the areas where the voice of the strongest can drown that of the weakest and the modes of thought and behaviour of a few can be imposed upon all the others. For this reason, peoples now aspire to make their voices heard – by acquiring the necessary technology and adapting it to their needs, thereby bringing about the genuine pluralism on a global scale.

*'I think it is wise nevertheless – and, in this, I am in agreement with the International Commission for the Study of Communication Problems itself – to see in this document **Many Voices – One World** not so much a conclusion as a starting point.'*

These words, spoken by UNESCO Director General Amadou-Mahtar M'Bow at the 21st UNESCO General Conference (Belgrade, 23 September–28 October 1980) are programmatic for this collection in more ways than one:

– the MacBride-Report* serves as the point of departure for a discussion as to the ways in which a connection can be established between the hitherto separate debates concerning the social relevance of new information technologies and the New International Information Order (NIIO);

* *Cf.* Sean MacBride (Chairman), *Many Voices – One World,* Report of the International Commission for the Study of Communication Problems, Paris, UNESCO, 1980.

- all contributions express – to a greater or lesser degree – a technological scepticism as defined in the Appendix to the MacBride Report by the two Latin Americans *Gabriel Garcia Marquez* and *Juan Somavia;*
- the entitlement of all peoples to equal right of access to information technology is the common basis of all articles, in accordance with their understanding of democracy.

From a political point of view it is by no means fortuitous that the contributions collected here are the result of initiatives taken by the Protestant Church. As emphasized in their articles by Sean MacBride and Helga Schuchardt, discussion of the NIIO and the related UNESCO policy is conducted in most western industrial countries on a superficial and distorted, even crudely anticommunist level. A further defensive strategy consists of hushing up these debates. It is in line with this taboo that those institutions officially responsible for these topics refuse to engage in a public debate. It has thus been only the Protestant Church which has regularly dealt with this subject in recent years in the Federal Republic of Germany. On a national level the Protestant Association for Media Communication organized the conference 'Information Pool or Information Monopoly' in 1977, as well as the conference on the NIIO in 1980.

The contributions presented here are the edited papers from an international conference held by the following Protestant and Ecumenical institutions: Protestant Academy of Arnoldshain (Schmitten, FRG), Protestant Association for Media Communication (Frankfurt, FRG) and the World Association for Christian Communication (London, UK). Implemented in cooperation with the Gustav-Stressmann-Institute (Bonn, FRG) and the Institute of Political Science of Marburg University (Marburg, FRG). The conference took place from 22 to 24 March 1982 at Godesberg Castle in Bonn-Bad Godesberg.

In his foreword to this book (originally a welcoming address and a contribution to the panel discussion closing the conference), *Sean MacBride* refers in particular to the increasing power of public opinion, contingent on the mass media. MacBride considers that its critical function is subject by two tendencies to growing danger: on the one hand, the state bureaucrats take more and more control of the media and on the other, a process of concentration and militarization is being implemented on the private sector in connection with all media. A similarly critical intent is behind the question raised by *Helga Schuchardt,* a committed Liberal Party development policy expert in the West German Parliament, as to whether the increasing internationalization of the media alone prevents more and more a democratic control: 'Although the information gathered on a worldwide scale constitutes a joint legacy of humanity, only few states have access to it – and that is those with the know-how and the capital. Those who monopolize information jeopardize a free media system because it becomes impossible.'

Jörg Becker, whose contribution concentrates on the North-South conflict, examines the effects of information technology on the Third World. He emphasizes the growing control from outside and integration in the capitalist world market, the increase in induced needs, the extremely unequal distribution within the Third World to the disadvantage of the greater part of the population and the dangers for cultural identities. *Cees Hamelink* makes it clear in his contribution that 'information technology is essentially a "convergence technology". More and more, it represents the indispensable infrastructures for the whole gamut of industrial production processes.' His discriminating suggestions for solutions in the North-South conflict are of particular interest. He recommends to the South a degree of separation off from the North, with intensified South-South cooperation, while suggesting to the North that it should only provide active 'assistance' when specifically requested by the South, and considers a technology moratorium as necessary for the North. In his paper, *Juan Rada* discusses the effects of microelectronics on the Third World. He points out that the problems of these new technologies have been virtually ignored in the major North-South reports of recent years, although in his view calling for a completely new concept of development policy. His main proposition refers to the progressive decline of the 'comparative cost advantages' of Third World in terms of low wages. 'Due to the application of microprocessors, microcomputers, alteration of products and processes, office automation and other changes, the productivity increase in industrialized countries is at or can potentially reach levels which are competitive with low labour costs,' Rada states.

Enrique González Manet sees in the present changes in information technology the new form of capital accumulation historically necessary to capitalism: 'If imperialism and neocolonial relations are going to be maintained under actual technological changes, the world needs to be linked to satellite and data banks and accept the imposition of the free-flow and free-access doctrine.' In his discussion of the political positions of the Non-Aligned Movement, the author draws attention to the latest changes in UNESCO. The fact that UNESCO officials have hels talks at Intelsat gives rise to his critical question as to whether this organization intends in future to be open to the private sector interests of the telecommunications industry.

In a critical review, *Neville D Jayaweera* elaborates the arguments in favour of the installation of satellites for the Third World, going on to compare them with the empirical reality of the present time. His conclusion is sobering; the expectations tied to the satellites have not been fulfilled anywhere. The author attributes this to the repetition in the present satellite technology of the modernism arguments of radio and tv technology in the 50s and 60s although these were already recognized as inadequate at that time: 'In the absence of structural reforms, both internationally and nationally (as set out in the programme for an NIEO and NIIO), satellites will most certainly benefit and strengthen the dominant interests, making the solutions even more difficult to attain.' In the closing contribution from *Noreene Z Janus*, the aspect finally becomes clear, referred to by a participant in the Bonn discussion as the 'missing link' to the other papers: the contents of the new information technologies are inevitably increasingly commercialized. The author is assuming that the new information technologies assist the advertising industry in achieving a greater precision in its sales strategies, and that it can with this technology implement greater access to foreign countries, in particular the Third World: 'The rapid installation of the new communications infrastructures suggests that the new "information age" will also be a "commercial age" at the global level.'

The wish repeatedly expressed at the Bonn conference for the development of alternative political strategies for the Third World is only partially met in these articles. This wish ranged from the demand for 'dissociation', covered the concept of a moratorium for information technology, and included the call to the countries of the Third World to commence as soon as possible with the drawing up of basic national plans for the mass media and information technology. The only partial development of alternative strategies is also dependent at the present time on the fact that there has not yet been sufficient analytical and empirical working out of the monstrous maze of dependency and causal relationships between information technology and international policy.

During the panel discussion at the end of the Bonn conference, Wolfgang Hessler, Protestant Association for Media Communication (Frankfurt, FRG), made the following suggestion. The World Council of Churches should be asked to examine the possibility of initiating a special programme, comparable to the anti-racism programme, for the detailed study of the threats and anxieties provoked by the new communication techniques around the world and for the preparation of quidelines for the social control of transborder data flow. And along these lines, the available results of the Bonn conference would also find their way into the General Assembly of the World Council of Churches (Vancouver, 7 July–10 August 1983).

Sean MacBride is to be endorsed in his view of the church as a moral basis for a policy critical of technology. Although the churches have never been free from dictates, they have always been able to maintain a certain degree of elbow-room in politics.

Contrary to the state and the private sector, the church has not subjected itself to the direct exploitation pressures of capital and technology. Creative use should be made of this elbow-room. And there are indications of a further consequence of this conference: As was reported during the panel discussion by Tran Van Dinh, Temple University (Philadelphia, USA), preparations are under way at the present time for a worldwide, interconfessional conference on Religions and New Technologies of Mass Communication in Asia in 1984 or 1985: 'My weapons against tv are "purifying" Buddhism and "liberating" Taoism.'

Jörg Becker
Priv.-Dozent, University of Marburg
Institute for Political Science

Preface

I have realized that for some reason the issues of communication as they relate to the Third World and to UNESCO have been more or less played down by the western press and the media in general. It is interesting that this matter has been investigated recently by the National News Council in the US, a body set up by the newspapers themselves to investigate the objectivity of the press. This Council notes that articles and news items about the International Commission for the Study of Communication Problems to UNESCO were distorted. What created this distortion was not editorialization in the writing but the selective process in which news reports were used. The first sifting out took place with the reporters' assessment of which developments were worthy of note. The process of excluding controversial material was then reinforced by the tendencies of the gatekeepers at the foreign desk in the newspaper offices at home to discard stories which did not highlight the conflict angle which they wished to highlight. The imbalance which characterized most news coverage in this country provided an inadequate foundation for independent judgment by Americans on the position their newspapers were taking in UNESCO communication issues. Equally troublesome, this imbalance set a poor example for the Third-World journalists and other sceptics on what they should find admirable as a model of prestige and immunity from government control in western journalistic expression.

So I am very glad that you are having this conference here to discuss the issues in a more balanced way. I am particularly glad also that this initiative has been inspired largely by the Lutheran Church. In my work both with regard to disarmament and to Namibia and the Human Rights, I have found that the Lutheran Church has never hesitated to take a courageous lead in these issues and therefore I would like to pay tribute to the leaders of the Lutheran Church for having taken this initiative in this case also.

The point I would like to make particularly at this stage is that there has been a change in the centre of gravity of power in the world from governments to public opinion, to the public sector. This has resulted from many different factors. The first was the increase in standard of education and the degree of literacy in the world. The second factor was the development of the media, electronic media in particular.

The electronic media has enabled news to be transmitted to every corner of the world instantly and in some considerable detail. This is also a new development. With regard to the electronic media, let me emphasize that by far the most important of the electronic media is the radio. Not because the radio is more persuasive but because it reaches areas of the world where there are no television sets. Television so far has been pretty well limited to large urban areas.

There are some 60 or 70 countries that have foreign radio news services. The 30 leading countries broadcast in a hundred different languages at the rate of 15,000 hours a week, which is a colossal output! In a hundred different languages, that means that the man in Laos, in Peru or in Zambia who is working in his village or his fields gets a news service in his own language from 10 to 20 different sources.

I think that in the future, foreign broadcasts in different languages are going to be one of the most potent ways of forming public opinion. And this is a part of the process I have referred to which has led to a change in the centre of gravity of power from governments to public opinion. If you have doubts about it you can take some countries as examples. The major example of this was the Vietnam war where for the first time in the whole history of the world a full-blown war – for the Vietnam war was a full-blown war – was ended in midstream without one side or the other having won it after public opinion in the United States and the rest of the world had said 'No!'. You have had other examples, in Iran recently. You may not like the regime in Iran that has been installed by Khomeini but the important factor to bear in mind is that here was the most powerful, cruel regime in the world which was overthrown by public opinion, by the people of the streets of Tehran. Public opinion overthrew a powerful regime that had the full backing and had been installed by the United States; public opinion was able to overthrow it in about the space of a month with very little bloodshed. Now we have the same kind of a thing happening in different parts of the world. I think the events in Poland are a result of the same process. The centre of gravity of power has been moving from the Communist Party, from the Government to the people. This process has probably been helped very considerably by the foreign news broadcasts. And I think this is a thing that our friends from the communist world should appreciate, that we have reached the end of an era in which the population can be insulated from what is happening in the rest of the world. I hope that the socialist countries will adjust to this situation, and adjust pretty rapidly. The events of Poland are only the tip of the iceberg.

Now, I thought it was useful to focus attention on the growing conflict which would develop between public opinion – if you like, the non-governmental sector – and the government. Governments are only beginning to realize this change in the centre of gravity of power and they will react very sharply against it. This means that there will be an increasing tendency to dominate the media, both the written media and the electronic media. Governments will more and more want to dominate it in an effort to control it and try to limit its power to inform people. In the western world the governments control the electronic media but have lost control over the written media to the same extent.

This question of concentration of the ownership and control of the media in the hands of multinationals requires urgent attention. There is a tendency of multinationals to insert a sense into the media. I think you have had this for some time in the Federal Republic of Germany but it is becoming more and more noticeable in France, Great Britain and many other countries. You have had this sordid spectacle in England: leading newspapers like *The Times, Sunday Times* and *Daily Times* being taken over by an Australian multi-national who already owns a number of newspapers in Australia, in the United States and in other portions of the globe. (I am referring to the purchase of the *The Times* by Murdoch). And what has been very interesting, too, is that despite all the assurances that had been given when *The Times* was bought by Murdoch, within a matter of a few months the editor was sacked, because Murdoch wanted to pursue a more actively right-wing policy.

You had the same thing taking place with *The Observer* in England. *The Observer* was first of all bought by an American oil company. And all kinds of assurances were given that there would be no interference with the policies of the paper. Within a matter of two years this oil field company sold the paper, without even telling the co-directors or the staff of the paper, to the Lonrho Company – the London and Rhodesian Finance Company, which was described by the conservative Prime Minister of Great Britain as the unacceptable face of capitalism. (It is an extremely shady company.) You have another worrying development, that is the purchase of publishing houses, and in some cases newspapers, by arms manufacturers. Arms manufacturers naturally want to be able to influence policies of governments so that they can sell more arms. And the concept of a world without arms, the concept of complete and general disarmament is detrimental to arms manufacturers. By beginning to buy different newspapers here and there, arms manufacturers want to promote the sale of arms, want to oppose disarmament.

In addition to the problem of concentration of the ownership and control of the media I would like to just mention two more areas of urgent concern:

newsprint shortage in Third-World countries, and efficient and cheap communication infrastructures, especially in Black Africa.

So – these are three small but important areas in which action could be taken. I think that they will require increasing attention. Now, what occurs to me really is the truth of what Albert Schweitzer pointed out many, many years ago: that man has lost the capacity to foresee and to forestall the consequences of his inventions. This is more obvious in the fields of communication than in other fields. We cannot deal with the issues of this conference properly if we divorce technology from morality because the two are closely linked. And this is the area where the role of the Church comes in.

The issues which face the world are largely based on moral questions, and I think we should try to understand it and try to give it a greater emphasis. We are living in a world in which we accept that governments are based on immorality rather than on morality which is an extraordinary reversal of what the concept used to be. Let me emphasize or give it on the line like this: heads of government, prime ministers or heads of states accepted bribes from various aircraft companies in order to sell their planes. And they were convicted of this; prime ministers, heads of states, generals and lesser important officials throughout the world. Nothing much happened about it. Most of the people continued to enjoy the fruits of the bribes which they received, and I do not think many of them ended up in prison. Another case in point is the problem of torture. In Amnesty International we found that between 40 and 50 governments use torture as a system of government; torture is used as a method of imposing government, of preventing opposition to the government. In different countries of Latin America maybe 50 or 100 students are taken in every week, tortured, kept in prison for two months and then released back to their relatives, so that they can tell the others what happened to them. The western world backed the torture regime in Rhodesia and the Salazar regime. It backed unbelievable things which happened in Vietnam, it is backing a regime in Kampuchea that massacred at least two million people. The western world installed the Shah of Persia who ran a terrifying dictatorship in Iran for 20 years.

The moral issues do not seem to count, and here surely we have a lesson to learn. One of the first tasks we have to do, is to look for some new moral basis. It could be that the Church should reinstall a moral basis for our societies.

Sean MacBride
President, UNESCO International
Commission for the Study of
Communication Problems

14

Information Technologies and the North-South Conflict

Helga Schuchardt, MP
President of the Board of Trustees
German Foundation for International Development

For a long time, media policy and the potential of new information technologies have been featured in international dialogue – the North-South dialogue in particular. However, they have hitherto only occupied the minds of a small circle of interested persons. So far, this topic has not found its way into official policy either in the west, in the east or in the south.

The question naturally arises in this context as to the real practical significance of reports such as the MacBride Report to UNESCO on the study of communication problems. In the Federal Republic of Germany, too, there is virtually no political discussion of this subject.

Speaking personally, I must admit that I willingly complied with the request to speak on this topic, not simply, for example, because I had already studied it in detail, but in order to force myself, as it were, finally to deal with it more comprehensively. Although I was already convinced of the importance of this sector, it had nevertheless become clear to me that it possessed a key function in the worldwide developments facing us in the near future.

We shall be unable to meet the challenges of our age or to shape the future without applying the media and modern information technologies.

We now have a wider-ranging knowledge of our future developments than ever before. Nobody can seriously call into question the trends outlined in 'Global 2000' or in the reports submitted by the World Bank, the UN or the Club of Rome. Any rational policy must take these trends into consideration. Yet, how can we reverse trends such as the population explosion and the destruction of our natural resources and of the environment in the relatively short time at our disposal unless we make optimal use of the media?

No rethinking process can take place without enlightenment. To that extent, a developed communications and information system ranks among our basic needs.

Science and politics have become more and more complex and the extent of specialization has grown accordingly. This has been accompanied by an 'atomization' of knowledge. The new information technologies permit us to join together the available specialized knowledge. Only new methods of communications can facilitate political decisions. But they are not used. By the same token, politics remain locked in specialization such as economic policy, environmental policy, development policy or media policy.

An integration of the available data renders the problems of the future so transparent that we simply cannot turn a blind eye to them in accordance with the motto: what cannot be, must not be. In other words, we cannot stick our head in the sand like an ostrich.

Today, the world could of course have a completely different appearance: we need only think of acid rain or the dying of forests and rivers. Yet, for the time being, we are behaving as if all this is not true. I feel sure that even the least sensitive of people will become aware of the problems – at the latest by the time his own house is affected.

Why am I saying all that in connection with this subject? If such a situation comes to pass – and that is probable – we shall need all the possibilities of modern communications in order to be able to carry out at very short notice the necessary measures.

A small illustration of how quickly a re-thinking process can take place may be seen from the success achieved in saving energy. Naturally, price trends and investment promotion have helped in this sector. But would this have been the case without the media?

The world's population now lies in the throes of a murderous struggle for a share of the available resources, and no end to this struggle is yet in sight. The current worldwide economic situation is inducing the rich and also the strong forces of the world's markets to adopt protectionist measures. It is all too natural for the strong states to use their power in order to prevent a recession from afflicting themselves and their citizens too much.

The persistent prevalence of the opinion that the First World can only provide active support for the development of the Third World if the former achieves economic growth may well be a realistic reflection of the facts. Nevertheless, this attitude still rests on a charity mentality: if only the rich countries remain wealthy, enough will be left over for the poor nations! To that extent, the North-South conflict still depends – perhaps again more than ever – on who gets the bigger share of the pie.

This bears considerable implications for information technology and its introduction on world markets. In the most highly developed countries, the media industries rank among the handful of growth industries. To start with, this is of course the case in the industrialized countries themselves: yet here, too, saturation-point will be reached within a foreseeable period of time as in other branches. This will set in motion competition for better marketing opportunities in the Third World. At the same time, the benefit for development will only play a subordinate role – if, indeed, any role at all!

Furthermore, the new technologies spring from a high level of technological know-how. It is not least due to the lead in information and communication technology that know-how has accumulated in only a few countries. Equally, the new media technologies are continuously increasing the differential in know-how and rendering it more and more insuperable.

In fact one of the main reasons for the North-South conflict lies in this differential in know-how. And to my mind, the trend in information technology resembles that in marine technology.

Admittedly, the oceans of the world are deemed the joint legacy of humanity. But this joint legacy is only accessible to a few countries, namely those able to provide the know-how and to raise the capital. Although the information gathered on a worldwide scale also constitutes a joint legacy of humanity, only few states have access to it – and that is those with the know-how and the capital.

It is particularly the industrialized countries dependent upon oil imports who are loud in their complaints about the power of the oil-producing countries. In my view, control of the media can pose a greater danger for humanity than control of oil. But as power almost automatically leads to abuse, the flow of information will only be permitted in such doses as correspond to the personal wishes of those who have the information at their disposal. Hence, it is small wonder that the call for a New International Information Order is becoming louder and louder.

Here, again, there is a parallel case in point. I am a convinced follower of free world trade. What gave rise to the call for a New International Economic Order? Surely it was simply because the strong countries in the market only permit free competition wherever it benefits them. If it harms them, they practise protectionism. It is not rare to find this leading to monopolies which in themselves destroy competition and free trade. In other words, the existing world economic order was brought into disrepute by its proponents.

The same observations apply to the international information order. Those who monopolize information jeopardize a free media system because it becomes impossible.

Where, for example, the MacBride Report is criticized by interested persons for having taken the interests of developing-country governments (including the totalitarian ones) too much into account – and this is undoubtedly true – the criticism mostly comes from those who have access to the media in the free countries and who often uncritically deem monopolies to be free institutions. Hence, we shall have to pay attention in order to ensure that the concept of freedom is not abused by avoiding or even eliminating undesired competition.

What chances and what risks are attached to the new media? The available information and the means of communication are marked by great variety. The media can stabilize oppressive systems and thus contribute to a preservation of power. The media have always served demagogues. However, the media are inviolable in the control of power. The knowledge of infringements of human rights throughout the world is only conceivable under a comprehensive system of information and communication, and a disclosure of such infringements is the first step towards combatting them.

Information and communication systems may lead to a society of total supervision, to men and women transparent like glass. Orwell's *1984* is now technically possible. However, these systems can be developed into an early-warning system with which to counteract negative trends in good time. They furnish an opportunity for a more sophisticated kind of forecasting and planning. Nevertheless, they could also mislead us into believing that everything can be planned.

Media systems may be abused for unilateral commercial interests, but they can also alter consumer habits to such an extent by the guidance they provide that our planet will remain inhabitable.

When misused, the new media may result in concentration processes, but they also meet the technical preconditions for breaking up monopolies by virtue of the possibility they give many people of obtaining access to the media 'even with small resources'.

Monopolization and supervision can destroy freedom. But the large number of possibilities can facilitate the delineation of the large number of opinions and enable the freedom of self-expression to become reality.

Whether or not the media in the widest sense of the term harbour risks or opportunities depends upon their right use.

One problem for me lies in the lack of willingness and ability among those who now supply material to the media to recognize that they are encouraging their abuse. Time and time again, we encounter expressions like objective, unprejudiced and balanced. But what do they refer to and who decides this? In short, the fact that information and communication systems are controlled by only a handful of people gives rise to scepticism.

What benefits can we derive in practice from the use of the media in the development process? I have already pointed out that the worldwide development in the population sector and in resources and environmental policy will not be controllable without the enlistment of information and communication technology. Let me now quote one example to illustrate how great the possibilities are of putting the media to use.

A few months ago, I went with a small delegation from the German Bundestag to Pakistan. That country must now cope not only with two million refugees from Afghanistan, but also with the three million head of cattle which they took along with them. These herds of cattle are literally eating their way through Pakistan. The devastating impact of this upon the vegetation, for example, is clearly visible to the naked eye. None of the afforestation programmes and *ad hoc* programmes for cultivating exploitable timber proves to be of any avail, or else simply remains a drop in the bucket unless accompanied by specific guidance programmes. These form the precondition for creating an awareness of the given problem and they bring about changes in the behaviour of the general public.

Diversity in the available facilities and flexibility in the use of media might well be the best way, after due consideration for living conditions and customs in the given country, to enter into a dialogue with the affected population and to find the right form of communication for permitting a positive and accepted trend and development.

However, a look at our efforts in the field of development aid reveals that these are also based on the various sectors. On the one hand you find afforestation projects and elsewhere media programmes. This could be applied equally to any other development programme. It does not take much imagination to visualize the value – and in particular the effective value – of a media component in projects relating to health, hygiene, nutrition, family planning and education.

Another point: What do we really know about the successes and failures of our efforts to develop a given region? Nothing! As a result, we repeat all our failures instead of avoiding them by *ad hoc* informational processing for the other programmes. It is particularly the failures which may exercise a positive effect upon the development process as a result of the correct use of media if only we are willing to learn from these mistakes.

The media in the service of projects and of programme work may render the development process much more effective, for the participants as well as for those affected. The media service acts as an informer, communicator and multiplier.

But if we take a close look at the problems throughout the world, we soon reach the conclusion that the requisite development process will, and indeed must take place even just for satisfying the basic needs – at a speed which will overtax the energies of all concerned.

We, the men and women of the developed world, have had lots of time to complete the concomitant rethinking process – at least to a certain extent. However, even in the industrialized countries, the speed of development is assuming such a dimension as to be constantly outpacing itself with the result that the negative consequences are no longer controllable. We need only think of the speed of structural changes in the economy and their catastrophic impact upon the labour market in our country, too.

Whether or not the people in the Third World are willing to accept the fact, they will not have so much time at their disposal.

We sometimes find ourselves confronted by the argument that the Third World cannot possibly make up in a short space of time for developments which took us 200 years to accomplish. Other people consider it progressive to argue that the countries of the Third World must retain their own mature structures. Needless to say, this may also be used to carefully mask the intention of retaining the present differential between rich and poor. Even though an uncoupling of the Third World may perhaps be desirable, this will not prove possible in practice.

A correct application of the information and communication systems in the Third World possesses eminent importance for the development of a country. If used correctly, they provide the sole opportunity of cushioning and determining the development processes in a rational manner.

So far, I have not mentioned the impact of new technologies such as microelectronics, data processing and telecommunications on the labour market. I only wish to refer to it in brief, because this subject contains enough material for a whole seminar. We know that 10 million jobs will be affected by the new technologies in the Federal Republic of Germany during the next 10 years and that a considerable percentage of these will be eliminated.

A large part of efforts in the Third World is directed towards the creation of work places. Nevertheless, these new technologies will mean – at least in the conurbations of the developing countries – that work places are destroyed before they have even been created. At the present time, nobody knows how to cope with these problems and I have no wish to arouse the impression that it has occurred to me what we should do. Nonetheless, this state of affairs reaffirms the perception that technology – wherever it stands at our disposal – will not be an end in itself, but must in fact serve the needs of mankind. Everyone will agree that this is self-evident. Yet when the situation calls for serious thought and for a clear statement that technology can therefore not be allowed to do everything it pleases and that decisions must occasionally be taken against its use, this attracts the attention of those who profit from its use. And hitherto, this has always been the stronger groups of society.

The information and communication systems wield less influence both internationally and nationally. The right to freedom of opinion and expression for everyone naturally only possesses theoretical character if the majority of men and women have no access to the media for expressing their opinion. Conversely, this proposition is only translated into reality when, if at all possible, everyone has access to the media.

The development of the world can only be carried out in a humanitarian manner if all peoples have an understanding for and about each other. Yet how do we obtain our knowledge of the Third World? Mostly from a journalist from an industrialized country assigned to the developing country who simply reports from the artificial world of his air-conditioned office or hotel room about a short trip to the country in question! However open-minded a western journalist may be, he will never prove able to report with the mentality of someone from his host country. That can only be done by a local journalist. Yet does the latter have access to the media with which this can be done? The official pronouncements by the governments will hardly be regarded as a substitute.

The concentration process in the news sector is now alarming. Even news agencies from industrial countries have fallen prey to the prevailing keen competition. The modest attempts by Third-World agencies to make their way are threatened by failure even before they have been able to become effective. Let us take the example of IPS, a Third-World news agency and a development project of the Federal Ministry for Economic Cooperation in the Federal Republic of Germany. To assist the viability of this news agency, it would be helpful for instance, if the Federal Press Office were to take out an annual subscription. However, this has not happened so far. I should add that this agency is in any case at risk on the international scene.

Yet anyone who demands a free flow of information can only demonstrate his honesty if this information does not remain a one-way flow, but is accompanied by efforts to promote it in both directions. Hence, the countries of the Third World must have their own infrastructure.

The developing countries ought also to think about regional integration. One of the reasons for the rise in Europe's significance vis-à-vis the superpowers lies in the fact that it has formed a community. For instance, if reports are written in Nigeria about Ghana, this information passes through the information filter in London. The wish to escape from this influence is something which really ought to evoke every possible effort by the developing countries.

There remain many topics which could be broached such as the East-West conflict, which is being transferred to the Third World, or the relationship between multilateral and bilateral approaches or the submission of a precise analysis about whose interests the media projects in the Third World are really intended to serve. Reasons of time prevent me from going into these subjects today.

But I would add two points. The complexity of the data-, information- and communication systems means that only a few people have access to them. This leads to an international differential of dependence stretching from the USA via Europe to the Third World and, of course, also to a national differential as between the state and the citizen or between large-scale industry and small businesses. In this context, I only wish to turn my attention to the international aspect. The more the media are internationalized, the more they will evade democratic controls.

What is the use, for example, of a national data protection law if the data disappear within an international network and may be retrieved whenever desired even though the law stipulates that they should long since have been erased! Or let us take another field. In the Federal Republic of Germany, we are proud of the fact that the competence for the media lies with the Länder so as to guarantee a decentralized autonomy. However, this deteriorates into a farce. For example, satellite-radio reduces national influence or even Länder influence to zero.

As it happens, it is the conservative members of society who do not find this all that alarming. Yet imagine the influence if, for instance, a country learns that advertising funds are best obtained by wrapping advertising spots within pornographic broadcasts. At any rate, the influence exercised on the quality will probably come to grief!

Every democratic-minded person must really be very interested in ensuring that such an important sector does not slip from democratic control.

Cooperation on development takes place – or at least ought to take place – in the interest of both sides. But these interests ought to rest on longer-term perspectives.

Cooperation on development which avoids resorting to the exploitation of short-term opportunistic economic advantages creates the confidence which is indispensable for long-term cooperation.

Furthermore, the Federal Government ought actively to support efforts capable of providing the developing countries with their own media structure even if this runs counter to its own interests in the medium term. A state commitment must be based on long-term aims and it must not fall prey to short-term market interests. Only that can legitimize state measures.

In my opinion, we must assume that no agreement will ensue about the non-use of the New Media. They will be used! Hence, our efforts can only be directed towards where and how they will be used so that they are not misused for the harm of the majority and solely for the benefit of minorities.

At present, the problem probably consists in the fact that the discussion on media policies will probably not produce any decisions, either nationally or internationally, until accomplished facts have been created. Those interested in a decision are not the people in possession of the media such as the industrialized countries and the media industry, but the developing countries and the consumers. Any blocking of decisions merely helps the monopolists.

At the beginning, I pointed out that these questions have still not found their way into policy-making. The important thing now is not so much to add more thoughts to the clever ideas already in circulation, but to consider strategies about how issues of genuine significance can gain appropriate weight in the field of policy-making.

New Information Technologies and International Politics in the 1980s*

Jörg Becker
Priv.-Dozent, University of Marburg
Institute for Political Science

Introduction

The current change in international relations has been essentially accelerated by the following two stimuli: It is on the one hand the increasing tendency towards the internationalization of capital, on the other hand the enormous momentum of technological innovation, not just in its rapidity, but above all new in its quality. Both trends show themselves in a clear-cut manner in the field of mass media and information technology. They are part of the electronics industry, a sector of industry which currently has the highest growth rate. Technological innovation and the internationalization of capital cannot be discussed separately especially in the field of information technology and the mass media: Whoever in the Federal Republic of Germany talks about optic fibre-cable systems, must be informed about the export interests of the glass-fibre industry to the Third World; or, whoever ponders upon tv-satellite projects for India cannot forget about the satellite plans of Radio Télé Luxembourg.

An analysis of these tendencies must take into account the following two premises: 1) the uniquely new quality of the current change in information technologies; 2) the values embodied in this technology.

The *novelty* of this change in information technology *does not* lie in our discovery of a diversity of new services, such as videotex, cable television, satellite transmissions or electronic mail. *Nor* does it lie so much in the rapidity with which the new information technology changes the personal and structural reality of our society. This novel quality can rather be emphasized by the two terms 'Telematics' and/or 'Compunications'. For the first time in the history of technology two formerly separate lines of development

* The author is grateful to Michael Lavin, Dublin and Frankfurt; and Bärbel Becker, Frankfurt, who translated this paper from German into English.

converge. This can be seen on the one hand by the technical development of the media towards telecommunications and on the other hand, under the influence of the microchip, the development of the adding machine towards the minicomputer. This 'marriage' of informatics and telecommunications is the qualitative novelty in current information technology.

There is an inbuilt tendency in this new system not to differentiate between scientific-technical and mass communication, between individually controllable and passively received communication, between print and electronic media, between acoustic and optical signal transmission, between information-storage, -processing and -transmission.

The totality of this new system implies the obsolescence of two further features of earlier information technology systems: the separation of place and time. With only a gap of seconds this all-encompassing network makes possible the universal dissemination of all possible information processes which have been developed until now anywhere on the globe. The future satellites – especially the technology of Direct Broadcast by Satellite (DBS) – are the last necessary link in the construction of this global network.

The future information systems are thus *global, independent of time,* linked together in *one single network* and most probably *intelligence-producing* (this description poses 'only' problems of definition). From this it must be clear that the problem of political power cannot be discussed only in traditional terms as the continuation of known dependency mechanisms. Also the form of political power which accompanies this information technology is qualitatively new. This new network of information technology is in economic terms not only explainable in the 'old' sense by the double character of 'information' as a commodity which not only has an intrinsic but also an exchange value, or that the visible and subliminal commercialization of communication increases worldwide, but mainly in the sense that all individual and social living conditions in the capitalist centres (work, free time, political power) can be seen more and more as dependent variables arising out of our immersion in information technology. This informatization of society has only superficially so-called positive or negative social effects. It is only a symptom to 'humanize' subsequently the 'inhumanity' of a workplace by a computer terminal, or to see optimistically in the two-way potential of regional cable-television systems the realization of participatory and grass-roots democracy. Social change is inherent in the informatization of society. Technology – information technology included – is not neutral, thus form and content correspond to each other; informatization itself (e.g. formalization, mediatization, quantification and finalization of human communication) is the essential expression of social change. To speak only of the social effects of informatization would mean to neglect the inherent characteristics of future society.

The *value system* of technology, my second premise, is very often ignored. The myth of the neutrality of technology is the more ominous and dangerous because it poses even more basic problems than the novelty of changes in information technology, and because a sluggishness on the part of scientists and followers of all political leanings has resulted in the assumption that one can differentiate between positive and negative consequences. The most recent example of this 'philosophy' can be found in the report of the Club of Rome on 'Microelectronics and Society'. The following is an example from Alexander King:

> *(Microelectronics) can be a blessing for mankind, because it can contribute to improving living conditions and abolishing poverty. But in the event that it is falsely used it can lead to the disintegration of society.[1]*

In this 'philosophy' of balancing negative with positive the technocratic socialist and the capitalist share the same perspective. One sees the solution to all problems in the control of technological development by the workers, while the other places his faith in the so-called market mechanisms which in the long run propel technology to a breakthrough in the interest of mankind. Although different in their political motivations, both positions resemble each other in that both are based only on consequences and uses of this technology and not on its inherent structure. In this context one can quote from the work *Die Antiquiertheit des Menschen* (The Antiquatedness of Mankind) of the Austrian philosopher Günter Anders which was published as early as 1954. In his chapter 'Kein Mittel ist nur Mittel' Anders attacks the maxim beloved by all parties, that what is important in technology is how we use it. The validity of this maxim is more than doubtful:

> *The freedom of controlling technology which it presupposes, as well as the belief that there are aspects of our world which are nothing more than 'means' to be continually linked to the achievement of 'good ends' is pure illusion. Means themselves are facts and these form us. We cannot escape the fact of their forming us, no matter to which end we put them, even though we might downgrade them to 'means' on the level of language. Our existence which is permeated with technology does not split into single, clearly demarcated stretches of road, of which parts are signposted 'means' while others are marked 'ends'. This division is legitimate only with regard to single acts and isolated mechanical procedures in industry, where the 'whole' is concerned; in politics or in philosophy it is not.[2]*

To be conscious about the value systems of technology does not imply a full-scale rejection of it. It should rather sharpen awareness of the necessity of rational planning processes in order to decide in a precise manner which kind and quality of social change as regards information technology is to be desired.

Information technology and the Third World

Considering the two premises of the novel quality of change in and the value system of information technologies, one has to examine in detail how this change has structurally affected the countries of the Third World until now. This shall be accomplished by using the following five categories laid down by Roy Preiswerk[3] as critical for the development of the Third World:

– foreign penetration;
– the relationship between intrinsic and exchange values;
– the regulation of need;
– the concentration of resources;
– identity.

1 Penetration dissociation from foreign penetration

If one discusses penetration taking satellite technology as an example, one has to be aware that the economic aspects of satellite technology cannot be reduced to the mere commercial possibilities of the satellite itself. This space segment in fact only constitutes a relatively unimportant part of a complicated and long technological chain. For example, Dornier, in a feasibility study of a South-American satellite system for the Federal Ministry of Development and Technology, calculated that the space segment constitutes less than a third of the total investment costs.[4]

Thus, satellite systems make possible in the first place an economic penetration of the Third World by way of the so-called follow-up business: earth stations, antennae, signal and amplification transmission systems, terrestrial cable networks, apparatus (tv, telephone, telex, etc.), cars, parts, buildings, fuel,for Diesel engines which are used in many rural areas of the Third World. The follow-up business constitutes in fact the main commercial possibility: The implementation of a pure information network certainly compels the adoption of the accompanying software, such as film, curricula, computer language, because these can be produced cheaper in the metropoles than in the peripheral countries, due to the lack of know-how and/or capital. For the same reasons the education and training of engineers, programmers, teachers and social scientists is carried out in the metropolitan context. The above-stated study by Dornier acknowledges this relationship; sometimes by way of implication, sometimes very openly:

A number of companies (in South America) are engaged in the production of television sets, mainly assembling parts which are delivered to them. . . However, one should not ignore the fact that part of the technical hardware would still have to be imported.

As a conclusion a (satellite-) test programme seems. . . useful, (because it) would strengthen the influence of German and/or European technology in South America.[5]

In the Dornier study for an African satellite it is put in more blunt terms:

The penetration and the consolidation of markets (in the field of telecommunication) is extraordinarily important for the future of the industry and the export-oriented nations. . . Seen from this background participation in a regional African communication satellite system is. . . naturally of interest. Being associated with the satellite system – which obviously profits from a certain sex appeal (sic!) – creates penetration possibilites into other fields bringing advantages for specific ranges of products.[6]

Whereas the above described mechanisms apply in the first place to news-satellite systems, other, however, similar mechanisms apply for weather- and remote-sensing satellites. These satellite systems, made meaningful only by data processing systems, can only come up to expectations, if they are fed an enormous amount of further information in addition to landsat data. There exist relatively little statistical data in the Third World, which also lack a time-series basis, and statistical methods are often not valid. Also, available data do not keep pace with the ever changing demands of planning. For all these reasons, remote-sensing by satellites in the Third World requires the construction of complicated computing systems. They contribute in an essential way to the fact that the Third World has become an ever increasingly important market for the leading computer manufacturers of the metropoles – General Electric (England), Fairchild (US), Advanced Micro Devices (US), Signetics (US), Motorola (US), Siemens (FRG), Thomson CSF (France) and Philips (Netherlands) – so that between 1972 and 1975 alone the export of computers to African countries increased by 44%, to Latin America by 38% and to Asia by 14%.[7]

Because the transfer of technology in these fields neither strengthens the domestic market for mass-produced consumer goods, nor contributes to the restructuring of an export-oriented national agriculture, information technology significantly contributes to a dependency on the global structures of capitalism. This connection lessens the national economic and political latitude of the respective countries of the Third World. The preceding analysis of transfer of technology fits into the various forms of service transfer between north and south which for a long period of time and to an increasing degree has resulted in a negative balance of accounts in services on the part of the Third World. Through this mechanism especially those countries of the Third World deficient in raw materials become ever more dependent on the industrialized countries; their balance of payment problems becomes ever more acute, their capability to meet the interest payments on their debts becomes ever smaller. A study of the Swiss company PROGNOS comes to the following conclusion in this context:

> *Within the framework of (UNCTAD estimates) it is supposed that expenditures for the transfer of technology will outpace the industrial production of the developing countries by 250%. . . It can be predicted with certainty that as developing countries increasingly industrialize, their expenditure for the commercial transfer for technology will rise proportionately and their respective dependence on the industrialized countries will also grow.*[8]

It is self-evident that economic dependencies have political consequences, which can be fully demonstrated by the two following examples. The Indonesian national news satellite system Palapa can with one push of a button be switched off by the American Department of Defence. A similar situation applied to the Iranian Intelsat link during the Iranian-American crisis 1979–1981. A US government study called for the termination of this link as one of several levels of escalation during this crisis. This would have rendered defunct the Iranian telephone- and television-system, the electronic fund transfer and flight reservations, and would have at the same time reduced the international reach of the Iranian telecommunication system by 70%.[9]

2 Intrinsic value/exchange value

Only when foreign penetration is discussed analytically and not in its concrete forms, can it be separated from the question of the interrelationship of intrinsic and exchange value. The worldwide capitalization of information implies everywhere the victory of exchange over intrinsic value: satellites and computer technology have hardly anything to do with their utilization potential within the national economies of the Third World, but rather with the transference value which the products of this technology gain in the form of money for foreign capital.

At this point one can make generalization that satellite technology is historically the last offensive on the part of the metropoles towards the peripheral countries: after the institutionalization of violence on a human level (slave trade, brain drain), on a material level (raw materials, energy resources) and on a commercial level (markets, import substitution) there follows now, as a result of this technology, a process of depriving the Third World of knowledge about itself. This can be made clear by the following example. Currently maps of the scale of 1:50,000 exist only for approximately 30% of the global surface, and such exact cartographic data is for the most part only of the industrial countries. For a great part of the Third World no maps exist and those that do are not suitable for planning purposes. The current surveying of the Third World by remote-sensing satellites has to be seen as an essential precondition and basis of the penetration of that which up until now has remained, either in full or in part, outside the exchange system. No matter whether population censuses, industrialization projects, planning of dams, opening up of raw material resources or the exploitation of forests, all projects which necessitate a high degree of functional planning including division of labour, specialization or professionalization and the necessary capitalization which runs parallel to these processes, become, as a result of this new satellite technology, not only more prevalent but also assume a different qualitative nature.

Remote-sensing satellites in general have to be seen as by far the most effective part of a new and very aggressive intellectual penetration of the Third World by the metropoles, which cannot afford any longer to base their offensive on prejudgment, ignorance, false or misinformation. The satellites are the modern linguists, anthropologists and missionaries who always have had the most detailed knowledge concerning microstructures in the Third World. Bearing in mind the observations of the Indian educationalist A K Jalaluddin, it is important to consider that not only are the excessive interests of western scientists in the study of such sensitive problems as religious and caste conflicts, ethnic, linguistic and group conflicts in developing countries examples of this intellectual penetration,[10] but that this is also true to an increasing degree for the satellites. The former collect 'soft data', while satellites collect 'hard facts' on a small, limited, regional and communal level. And thus it is not by coincidence that the UN Committee for the Peaceful Use of Outer Space discussing the question of prior consent on the part of the countries subject to satellite photography concentrated among other issues on the size of the reduction potential of the photographs.

How little intrinsic value the photography of the remote-sensing satellites has for the economies of the Third World can be demonstrated using the example of the satellite storm-warning system in Bangladesh. It is only superficially true that in 1979 the lives of thousands of people were saved because of the early detection of a cyclone over the Bay of Bengal. Bangladesh is one of the 25 poorest countries on earth: 500 people inhabit one square kilometer, the per-capita income of the population of which 90% are peasants is US$80 per year, 10% of the population possesses 40% of the total ground. It is estimated that 80% of the population lives below subsistence level, which means their income docs not provide for the bare necessities, such as food, shelter, clothing, education and health care. When one takes into account that only in approximately 100 urban and semi-urban areas of Bangladesh there is adequate shelter, tap water, health- and community services, then it is boardering on cynicism to emphasize the advantages of saving lives through the early storm-warning. To put it differently: For the mass of Bangladeshi the intrinsic value of this early-warning satellite is of an extremely ambivalent nature; given the already sub-human standard of living, their bare physical survival led to a greater intensity of human misery.

3 Basic needs/induced needs

'(Satellite technology) will be increasingly necessary in adapting human needs to the limited possibilities of our globe.'[11] This conclusion, arrived at by one of the many scientists involved in the Landsat programme, should be considered less as a Freudian slip than as an unwitting but correct perspective in the relationship between man and high technology. It lies in the nature and internal dynamic of such technologies that – in keeping with their economic realization principle – they must create new needs, to which the user only later adapts after a period of appropriate conditioning. To orientate satellite technology towards the needs of humanity, thus demanding the reversal of the technocratic principle, would be the first step in the direction of a need-orientated development strategy. However, its necessary precondition would be the active and participatory involvement of those affected by this technology and thus a strengthening of the intrinsic value and a reduction of extraneous influences which is definitely not the case either in the Third World or with regard to the consumers in the metropoles.

Satellite technology strengthens what Joseph Ki-Zerbo described as muteness in relation to the activities of the monopolized news agencies. When, without the possibility of its rejection, a country is overwhelmed by foreign infor-mation, not being able to present one's own images and information, then one is mute. This means that one must assume a passive role serving the basic needs of others. 'The capacity for communication is one of the essential characteristics of mankind. A mute country has no sovereignty.'[12]

4 Concentration/distribution of resources

In the domestic as well as the foreign political sector the question of how available resources are distributed has to be regarded as essential to the evaluation of the degree of democratic potential in a specific sector; this is true for the production sector of the respective resources as well as for the regulations governing their use. It may well be that one of the current most dominant myths is that the future forms of telecommunication and information technology make possible social decentralization processes that they provide for mass participation, if not in the production of the technology, then at least in its decentralized utilization.

This has to be opposed first of all in general terms. The increasing automatization of every sector of life has resulted in an ever increasing complexity and intertwining of effects which favour a centralization of power, decisions and control in the economy as well as in private and public institutions. This historical tendency is especially true of the information technology sector.

The involvement in the production of the new resource information technology is dependent on an immensely high capital investment which with regard to satellite technology or overall optic fibre-cabling goes into billions, thus limiting it from the beginning to transnational corporations and/or state bureaucracies. Participation of socially competing groups, such as the production sector, the middle class, single-interest groups or agriculture, which is deemed necessary even by liberal democratic standards is thus already initially excluded from this rapidly expanding industry. The politically and economically preexisting advantage of the transnational corporations and state bureaucracies increases manifold. 'Whoever has possessed before the capacity for knowledge, control and decision-making ('power'), can multiply it now automatically and (through telecommunication) can disseminate it to any chosen place.'[13]

This extraordinary concentration of power is even more strongly apparent in the relationship between the industrialized and the developing countries, as will be demonstrated by two short examples. When Intelsat tried to convince the African states at the end of the 60s and beginning of the 70s to link up with this international satellite system, they promised that this would lead to a greater connection between the remote areas and the centres as well as to a strengthening of inter-African exchange. The aeronautics company Dornier, however, stated in 1980: 'These stations have contributed little to the improvement of the inter-African telecommunication system, because they mainly replaced the old HF-connections to the former mother countries.'[14] In other words, satellite technology has only made more effective the already existing centralization of power in the native bureaucratic class and the foreign metropoles which cooperate with it. A further empirical example can be drawn from the study comparing Algeria and El Salvador undertaken by Harvard University. Here the effects of satellite and information technology on two culturally and politically extremely different peripheral societies were examined. The implementation and use of this technology has in both countries led to an increased centralization of decision-making processes.[15]

Even when the apologists of the new information technology would admit to the centralization, concentration of power and control of information within the production sector, they still mostly point to its decentralized use. There emerges the image of the user whose involvement in this technology is directed by his own individual needs and the image of the Third World which, through decentralized access to the data banks of the industrial countries by means of satellite transmission, can draw all information relevant to its own needs. This also is a myth. Although decentralized access to the large information systems is possible, it is still dependent on the filter-, selection-, decision- and control mechanisms which emanate from one control centre. It is not the decentralized access possibilities to the overall system which are the decisive features of the system; the reverse is true: it is the centre which ensures its access possibility to the periphery.

Thus the utilization of this technology only seems to be decentralized. However, there is a further mechanism with regard to use and reception which can give prominence in power and information as well as in the access to knowledge. This is the capacity to transform the available data into decision-making knowledge and the possibility to gain prominence from this knowledge which is only within the capability of few participants to realize. Within the Third World only three groups profit from this knowledge and its consequent possibilities: 1) transnational corporations which deliver the technical products; 2) transnational banks which finance the import and installation of these technologies; and 3) the new bureaucratic class in the centres of the Third World.

As one can already observe an increasing knowledge gap due to the increasing availability of mass media information – those already educated make better use of the enlarged supply, whereas those kept ignorant fall further behind in their standard of information – so likewise with information technology an increasing data gap has developed. The gap between those with and those deprived of information widens; the centralization tendencies in the metro-pole-periphery-model grow.

5 Identity: conservation/loss

Satellite technology is in a way the pinnacle of information technology, the technological spearhead in the socio-psychological penetration of Third-World cultures. This manifests itself in various respects. As a part of a vast chain of technology, this part of the electronics industry contributes to the development of social differentiation, and that means internal alienation. Extreme forms of division of labour, specialization, professionalization, education and training will be the accompanying effects of this technological drive. At the same time the self-colonization process is promoted by the importation or manufacturing on an import-substitution basis of goods for production or consumption by this technological chain. But to my mind more important are those two mechanisms which can be called the *weakening* and the *homogenization* of Third-World cultures.

The era of colonialism and imperialism can in some ways be characterized by the aggrandizement of the metropoles with cultural goods, i.e. European museums were stuffed with cult objects, artworks and mundane goods, likewise the remote-sensing satellites pilfer non-material goods from the Third-World, namely knowledge and information of itself. These are stores of knowledge which constitute the state of the Third World itself, but for which it cannot or will not have any systematic access possibilities. The systematic knowledge about the Third World thus becomes ever more thorough and intensive outside of it. The manifold possibilities for external control, created in this way, will reduce the cultures of the Third World into a functional variable in technological planning processes. The diversity of the human element enriching different cultures will be sucked dry.

Parallel to this drain of cultural identity the international news satellites, especially the projected DBS, contribute to a reversed mechanism which is the cultural penetration from without. Even at this time, through the 'traditional' media, such as books, press, television and partly the radio, the Third World is exposed to an extreme and one-sided information flood from the metropoles. The contents of the western mass media have already promoted cultural disintegration and identity conflicts within the Third World (even when there is little empirical knowledge on the concrete process of absorbing these messages). The global intercabling of all entertainment media and their software which is now made possible by news satellites will expose the cultures of the Third World to an ever greater cultural pressure.

The two possibilities of satellite technology, the draining of knowledge together with the dissemination of western values and norms in the Third World, will strengthen and accelerate to a great degree the loss of cultural identity in the developing countries.

Possible resistance strategies

It would be an illusion to hope that the above described mechanisms of intensified linking of the peripheries to the metropoles by information technology could be changed on a short-term basis, because the structural laws of the internationalization of capital, the uncontrollable proliferation and the 'cancerous' and uncontrollable dynamics of technological innovation oppose it. Whereas in the US the Carter Administration showed at least on a diplomatic level and in negotiations some willingness to compromise with the Third World, without ever being able to grant any concessions, the administration under Reagan returned to a clear-cut and outspoken opposition to all demands for change, for the beginnings of the realization of a New International Information Order. This can be demonstrated for example by the objection of the US and Israel – against all other nations – to the acceptance of a UNESCO resolution on media politics which was brought before the General Assembly of the United Nations in December 1981.[16] It is also apparent in the hostile contributions on the media politics of UNESCO to the Committee on Foreign Affairs of the House of Representatives;[17] furthermore in the behaviour of the North-American delegation at the meeting of the International Council of the International Programme for the Development of Communication (IPDC) in Acapulco, January 1982; as a consequence the US together with Japan and the Federal Republic of Germany have refrained until now from any direct financial contribution to this special UNESCO programme.[18]

The Reagan Administration – realizing the growing competition from Europe – has clearly recognized the increasing importance of the peripheral markets for its own satellite and telecommunication industry. Thus, the US Agency for International Development recently received the sum of US$25 million to establish a rural satellite programme in the Third World; an initiative which is being promoted as advancing the living standards in rural areas of this part of the Third World.[19] In reality it fulfills experimental and market penetration functions.[20] This rural satellite programme will cooperate closely with Intelsat. The Reagan Administration will give greater support to Intelsat than it has done up until now, because only a strong, centrally operating satellite organization such as Intelsat could guarantee that the political pressure from the Third World for a new distribution of frequencies and orbit positions would not increase.[21]

On the ideological level the administration supports not only to a greater degree the protection of the principle of the 'free flow of information', but in addition actively supports the rights of the industrial countries to an unhindered and free access to the telecommunications infrastructure inside the Third World. Seen on its own terms this is more than logical, because information technology means essentially the securing of economic advantage through the follow-up industries. Also argued from a technological point of view such a strengthening of the 'free flow of information' doctrine is near at hand. The increasing interconnection between tele- and computercommunication has rendered obsolete an unequivocal distinction between information-input, which under prevailing opinion is governed by the international legal principle of the 'free flow of information', together with the information processing and information-output, which under prevailing opinion are governed by the national legal systems of sovereign states. Consequently, in the opinion of the metropoles, the unhindered access to the information infrastructure of the peripheral countries must, politically and legally, be guaranteed. It is only in this light that the following recommendation issued by the US State Department in August 1981 can be understood:

> *(It is recommended) to enlarge acceptance of the principle of the free flow of information and ideas,* **including acceptance of the applicability of this principle to newly emerging communications and information technologies.**[22]

In spite of this new pressure there are various weaknesses and inconsistencies in the chain of these dependencies as well as political forces which can counteract the above described tendencies and which in different and changed historical circumstances can exert their influence.

1 On the part of the Third World the politics of the *Non-Aligned Movement* must be seen as the most potent force for resistance in this area. Since the beginning of the 70s the themes of mass media and information technology have played an ever increasing role at their summit conferences. However heterogeneous this movement seems, they are united in their demand for the decolonization of the mass media and information technology. As the linking

of the peripheries to the metropoles will increase through projected satellite technology and not decrease, the common protective interest of the non-aligned countries will be homogenous enough to be effective as a political weapon. A few countries of the Third World have in the meantime managed relatively well to dissociate themselves from the world market in certain areas of information technology. Thus, for example, Algeria has prohibited the transborder data flow from computer to computer, because it does not see any possibility of regulation and control. Also the Indian satellite technology programme has managed to achieve relative autonomy. India, as one of the seven countries engaged in space development, can independently build its ground stations, 40% of its satellites and 70% of its rockets. These relative dissociations have, however, no international political parallel, but *national dissociation* can be the first necessary step towards developing a strategy of resistance.

2 The countries of the Third World can build up further resistance potential through the application of the *strategy of multilateralization* in UN bodies. This strategy has in the past few years been relatively successfully applied. On the *political* level the Third World must continue to actively resist the doctrine of the 'free flow of information', because this principle legitimizes the current structure of metropole-periphery relations. On the *technological* level the doctrine of 'first come, first served' held by the International Telecommunication Union with regard to the distribution of radio frequencies has to be abolished. This principle always serves the interests of the technologically most developed countries. On the level of *international law* the Third World must uphold its right of 'prior consent', which means prior consent to remote sensing and satellite transmission of the affected country. Especially the aspect of international law concerning remote-sensing by satellite or DBS in all events must not be subjected to the unlimited principle of the 'free flow of information', as it is interpreted as international law in the Federal Republic of Germany. The following international treaty agreements deal more thoroughly with the foregoing issues: the International Radio Treaty, League of Nations, 1936; the clause in the First International Space Treaty, UN 1961, which states that 'the exploration and use of outer space should only be for the betterment of mankind.' This implies the rejection of the advantage of any one party; Resolution 428A of the International Telecommunication Union, 1977, which says that spill-over by satellites is allowed only by the prior consent of the affected countries; the basic principles of international cooperation.

3 Finally, there are further political possibilities for resistance in the behaviour of the *Common Market countries*. These countries have long since,

out of a fear of American economic competition, realized that the unhindered development of satellite and information technology drives them into a variety of dependencies on the US. Possible agents of Western European resistance strategies are the national PTTs, the Council of Europe and some national governments which, like the French and the Swedish, though for different reasons, become ever more conscious of their foreign political dependencies.[23]

4 The growing informatization of international relations will in addition intensify the *structural conflict between transnational corporations and nation states*. Already now many state-controlled bodies in developed countries find themselves in the awkward situation that the quality of decision-making knowledge possessed by transnational corporations is by far superior to their own. This conflict could be intensified by another historical tendency, namely the growth of national consciousness in the Third World.

5 In the monetary sphere the increasing informatization of international relations is currently inhibited most by recession, budgetary imbalance and the *impending collapse of the international credit system.*

6 Technological and infrastructural conditions hinder total informatization now as before. One of the essential preconditions for penetration of the Third World by means of information technology is up until now in many cases only partially existent, that is a fully developed *infrastructure*. Without an electricity supply, a stable electrical current or continually functioning telephone system, to name only a few of the everyday necessities missing in the Third World, it is only partially possible to implement information technology systems. In the societies of the peripheral countries it is most probably still impossible, due to their infrastructures, to gather valid individual and social data. But it is just this validity which is a necessary precondition for automatic data processing. Currently all programmes fed with population data from the Third World are in danger of producing false analyses. The input of non-valid data multiplies many times the occurrence of inaccuracies in complex computing processes.

Because of this deficient infrastructure the extremely unequal access to information technology within the Third World will probably in the long run develop into their *subtlest means of defence*. The centralization tendencies of the new technologies give perhaps enough time and space to the marginal populations to become conscious of and to organize their own indigenous means of defence.

7 Further difficulties result from specific characteristics of information technology systems which can be named after their formulator the 'Weizen-

baum' effects,[24] The input of non-valid data into computer programmes poses a more profound problem than non-valid population data in the Third World. In the industrial countries as well forecasts are frequently computed on the basis of non-valid data. Considering for example that large research teams work on an exclusively theoretical level to deduce certain macroecenomic relevant indices and, furthermore, that these various theoretical schools are in conflict with each other, then there is hardly any reliable criteria left to determine which data are to be used and which are not. Weizenbaum predicts an additional development. Data processing systems have only existed for the past 20 years, so that the long-term effects of the accumulation of non-valid data have hardly made themselves felt. According to Weizenbaum, it is only a question of time until the cumulation of 'dirty data' produces such grave miscalculations that misplanning in business and bureaucracies will have reached such dimensions that they are obvious to everybody.

References

1 Alexander King, 'Mikroelektronik und globale Interdependenz' in *Auf Gedeih und Verderb,* Mikroelektronik und Gesellschaft, Bericht an den Club of Rome, edited by Günter Friedrichs and Adam Schaff, Vienna, Europaverlag, 1982, p 352.
2 Günther Anders, *Die Antiquiertheit des Menschen,* Vol 1, Über die Seele im Zeitalter der zweiten industriellen Revolution, 5th and revised edition, Munich, Beck, 1980, pp 99.
3 Roy Preiswerk, 'Kulturelle Identität, Self-Reliance und Grundbedürfnisse', in *Das Argument,* 120/1980, pp 176.
4 Gerhard Rausch and Hans Löhle, *Kommunikationssatelliten für Südamerika,* Bonn, Der Bundesminister für Forschung und Technologie, 1979, p 9.
5 *Ibid.,* pp 62 and 139.
6 Wolfgang Kriegl and Wilfried Laufenberg, *Kommunikationssatellitensystem für Afrika,* Bonn, Der Bundesminister für Forschung und Technologie, 1980, p 64.
7 *Cf.* Cees Hamelink, *ECDC/TCDC, The Role of Telematics,* Paper presented at the International Workshop on the Promotion of Economic and Technical Cooperation among Developing Countries in Bled, Yugoslavia, 2–7 November 1981, p 9.
8 Christel Bergmann and Helge E Grundmann, *Aussagen zur Interdependenz zwischen Industrie- und Entwicklungsländern,* Gutachten im Auftrag des Bundesministers für wirtschaftliche Zusammenarbeit, Basel, Prognos AG, 1979 (mimeo), pp 13.
9 *Cf.* Herbert I Schiller, *Who Knows: Information in the Age of the Fortune 500,* Norwood, Ablex, 1981, pp 110.
10 Interview with the author in April 1980 in New Delhi.

11 R Mühlfeld, 'Bilanz über den Einsatz der Satellitenfernerkundung in den Bereichen Geologie/Lagerstättenkunde, Hydrologie, Bodenkunde/Landnutzung im Rahmen von Projekten der Bundesanstalt für Geowissenschaften und Rohstoffe' in *International Archives of Photogrammetry,* Vol XXIII, Part B8, Commission VII/1980, p 652 (italics by the author).

12 Joseph Ki-Zerbo, 'Unterricht über die Dritte Welt und die Probleme ihrer Entwicklung' in *Die Dritte Welt in Schule und Jugendarbeit,* edited by Jörg Becker, Frankfurt, Haag & Herchen, 1980, p 20.

13 Wilhelm Steinmüller, 'Informationstechnologie-Folgen' in *Nachrichten für Dokumentation,* 6/1981, p 249.

14 Wolfgang Kriegl and Wilfried Laufenberg, *Kommunikationssatellitensystem für Afrika, op.cit.,* p 22.

15 *Cf.* John H Clippinger, *Who Gains by Communications Development?* Studies of Information Technologies in Developing Countries, Cambridge, Harvard University, Programme on Information Technologies and Public Policy, 1976 (mimeo) (working paper 76–1).

16 *Cf.* United Nations General Assembly, Thirty-sixth session, Agenda item 67, Documents A/36/819 and A/36/PV.100, 12 & 16 December.

17 *Cf. Review of US Participation in UNESCO,* Hearings and Mark-up before the Sub-committees on International Operations and on Human Rights and International Organizations of the Committee on Foreign Affairs, House of Representatives, Ninety-Seventh Congress, First Session on H. Res. 142, 10 March, 9 and 16 July 1981, Washington, US Government Printing Office, 1982. (*Cf.* especially the contribution by Elliott Abrams).

18 *Cf.* Peter Schenkel, *Kurzbericht über das zweite Treffen des Zwischen-staatlichen Rates des Internationalen Programmes für die Entwicklung der Kommunikation,* Quito, CIESPAL, 1982 (mimeo).

19 *Cf. Uplink,* Newsletter of the Rural Satellite Programme, 1/1981.

20 *Cf.* Dennis R Foote (leading member of the Stanford University Programme), *Overview and Assessment of Satellite Communications Systems for Education and Development,* Presentation to the UN Regional Seminar on Satellite Communications for Education and Development, March 1981, p 16.

21 Office of the Undersecretary of State for Security Assistance, Science and Technology, *International Aspects of Communications & Information,* Draft of 4 August 1981 (mimeo), p 23.

22 *Ibid.,* p 5.

23 *Cf.* Jörg Becker. 'L'Europe et le Tiers-Monde dans la bataille d'information' in *Le Monde Doplomatique,* Janvier 1982, pp 8–9.

24 *Cf.* his following works: Joseph Weizenbaum; 'Der Einfluß von Computern auf die Gesellschaft' in *Psyche,* Vol XXIX (1973), pp 171–183; Joseph Weizenbaum, *Computer Power and Human Reason,* From Judgment to Calculation, San Francisco, Freeman 1976; Joseph Weizenbaum; 'Once More: The Computer Revolution' in *The Computer Age: A Twenty-Year View,* edited by Michael L Dertouzos and Joel Moses, Cambridge and London, MIT Press, 1979, pp 439–458.

Information Technology and International Relations: Perspectives for South and North

Cees J Hamelink
Institute of Social Studies, The Hague

Significance of information technology in international relations

In the debate on the role of technology – and particularly its transfer – in international relations, information does not usually figure very prominently. Attention tends to focus on such sectors as medical, pharmaceutical, agricultural and manufacturing technologies. Also, international development agencies generally give low priority to information technologies, such as those related to telecommunication networks. Throughout the 1970s, for example, less than 2% of the budget of the Inter-American Development Bank was allocated to telecommunications. During the period 1971–75 the World Bank allocated an average 4% of its loans to telecommunication projects. In 1980 the World Bank and its affiliated International Development Association directed US$131 million or 1% of total loans, to loans for telecommunications. Western private financiers have shown interest in telecommunications only when good rates of return could be expected. This has biased funding towards the installing and upgrading of urban facilities and inter-urban routes rather than towards networks that cover rural areas.

Information technology, however, deserves considerable attention, for the following considerations.

a) Transfer of technology is basically transfer of knowledge/information. As the preamble to the UNCTAD Draft International Code of Conduct on the Transfer of Technology states: 'transfer of systematic knowledge for the manufacture of a product, for the application of a process, or for the rendering of a service.'

Technology is information represented by models, diagrams, plans and formulae embodied in studies, training programmes and equipment, and transferred through sales and licensing of patents and via technical experts.

At heart, technology transfer is the transmission of information and, as such, is dependent upon the technology that provides the appropriate mechanisms: information technology. The volume and structure of technology transfer are intrinsically related to the presence and quality of information infrastructures. The development of technology at large is also dependent upon those infrastructures, which facilitate technological innovation through the exchange of data, the remote processing of data, simulation exercises, and distribution networking for joint research.

b) The International Patent System essentially has an information function. It is intended to stimulate technological progress via dissemination of information about inventions.

c) In the transfer of technology, information is a crucial factor in agreements between contracting parties. In recent drafts of the Code of Conduct on the transfer of technology, both the acquiring and the supplying party are obliged to disclose information relevant to the particular transfer and use of the technology under negotiation.

d) Information technology can rightly be called 'the command and control system' for all other technologies. The control of information technology is a vital component in the distribution and execution of social power. Differential access to such technologies as implied in data processing and telecommunication determines differential access to the capacity to collect, process and use information: a conclusive factor in social decision-making. The struggle about the control over information technology in society is essential, because the outcome will determine how decision-making power will be distributed and hence how all major social decisions will be made. Social decision-making will affect the development and application of the whole range of technologies.

e) Information technology is essentially a 'convergence technology'. More and more, it represents (particularly through the integration of data processing and telecommunication technologies) the indispensable infrastructure for the whole gamut of industrial production processes. All these become increasingly information-extensive. Rapid developments in microelectronics technology in particular, will bring industries to realize that the volume and differentiation of their production are determined by the application of highly advanced information technology. In its applied form (e.g. microcomputers, robots) that technology will largely replace the factor unskilled and semi-skilled labour, and will define skill requirements on the level of high-technology management.

The 'convergent' nature of information technology also implies strong industrial concentration. Formerly separate fields such as data processing, text processing, information storage, photocopying and information transmission, are increasingly integrated through the merger of technologies and can be operated by a single, vertically integrated corporation.

f) Advanced information technology is 'synergetic', i.e. growth leads to growth in many other industries. It creates an infrastructure around its products and services, similar to the automobile earlier in this century.

As with the transition from agriculture to industrial manufacturing, today's shift to the information industry spawns a scale of new industries, such as software production, processing services, timesharing facilities, semiconductor manufacturing, telecommunication operations, data base management, electronic publishing, and legal services for software copyrighting.

g) Information technology is a spearhead technology. The US National Association of Manufactures has stated:

> *The indications are that the information technology sector will be critical for the United States as it faces the intensely competitive world economic situation for the 1980s. Our world leadership in this field will benefit American trade directly, through the export of goods and services in this sector itself, and indirectly, through improving the competitive efficiency of US companies worldwide in all sectors.*

And as Charles Lecht, President of the Advanced Computer Techniques Corporation, has claimed. 'There is little doubt the *entire* US economy will be adversely affected if we manage to lose the decisive position of strength and leadership we now hold in computer technology.'

At a hearing of the 'US House of Representatives Sub-committee on Government Information and Individual Rights, Assistant Secretary of Commerce Harry Geller stressed the vital importance of US exports in telecommunication and other information goods. 'Telecommunications and information merchandise exports represented 10% of the overall US merchandise exports in 1977.' In worldwide trade the contribution of the computer and telecommunication industries amounted to some 10% in 1980. In the past few years, advanced information technology has attracted several large new entrants to the field, including Exxon, Boeing, Matra and Volkswagen.

The production and distribution of advanced information technological products and services ranks after energy, automobiles and chemicals as the fourth largest industry in the world. In 1980 it had an approximate turnover of US$100 billion.

h) Another consideration is that R&D investments in information technology exceed similar investments in other industrial branches, due particularly to its short product cycles and to the rapid obsolescence of its products. In 1977, the combined average percentage of sales spent on R&D for US satellite, data processing and electronics was 4.1% compared to 2.5% in another R&D-intensive industry, chemicals. In 1979 R&D expenditures in the US data processing industry were considerably larger than in all manufacturing, amounting to 7.5% of total turnovers. This figure increased slightly to 7.6% in 1980.

In the Federal Republic of Germany in 1978, the electronics industry spent over 6% of sales on R&D, comparing with 4.7% in chemicals, 5.7% in automobiles, and 3% in engineering and mining. Some leading West German firms spent more than this, e.g. Siemens with 10% and AEG/Telefunken with 7% of total turnover. On a global scale, R&D expenditures on information technology are estimated at some30%ofthe world R&D budget.

i) Information technology is the chief architect of the infrastructures through which the values of the transnational business system are spread globally. The instantaneous and massive distribution of information which it facilitates, permits the persuasive introduction on a global scale of life styles, consumption models and social structures which are linked with a very advanced level of development and which are very deceptive for societies which are barely able to survive.

Information technology also plays an important role in the cultural synchronization of the world and contributes strongly to the consolidation of transnational commercial interests.

Information technology and South-South relations

The paucity of South-South information traffic is a serious obstacle for horizontal forms of cooperation among developing countries. Most international information routes, be they telephony, mail or shipping, still reflect colonial times and link the countries of the south only via the north. Recent gatherings on cooperation among developing countries have recognized this.

The United Nations Conference on TCDC (1978 in Buenos Aires) declared as one TCDC objective the increasing and improving of 'communications among developing countries, leading to a greater awareness of available knowledge and experience as well as the creation of new knowledge in tackling problems of development.' The UNDP has responded to this objective with the proposal for an interregional Development Information Network (DIN). The feasibility study for DIN, undertaken by the Third-World agency Inter Press Services, states that 'a new flow of information, with distinct characteristics, can be created through a computer-operated South-South network, providing a full horizontal exchange of mutually supportive development information.' DIN is a promising plan that so far still remains on the drawing board.

Also the High-Level Conference on Economic Cooperation among Developing Countries in Caracas (May 1981) emphasized the crucial role of information exchange and communication capacity among developing countries. Regarding technology, the Conference recommended, 'establishment of networks of scientific and technological institutions for mutual benefit and to facilitate harmonization of strategies and programmes through the exchange of information and experience in the field of scientific and technological development.'

Again, it is clear that information technology is the convergence technology: the basic component of South-South cooperation. Information technology will have to provide the infrastructures through which: technical knowledge/ information is produced, processed and transferred, research and development can be shared, joint data banks can be established, resource data can be collected and processed, and financial intelligence can flow. Design and implementation of such networks could be undertaken through joint ventures, among developing countries.

In the NIEO and NIIO debate the need for horizontal information networks has been recognized.

In fact, however, it has to be observed that, in spite of some initiatives such as Inter Press Service, the African news exchange (PANA) and Caribbean news exchange (CANA), the fundamental structural transformations which were projected have not been achieved. It should be questioned, therefore, in how far this failure is caused by shortcomings and inconsistencies of models and strategies implied in the 'new international order' proposals. The new international order claims sovereign control over national economic and non-material resources. However, this does not make a country less dependent. But the country has the power to bargain with its resources. This presupposes the building of countervailing power by dependent countries. In effect, such power would have made it possible for developing countries to enter international negotiations with reasonable chances of success. Apart from the oil producers' cartel, no effective bargaining power has been created among the developing countries during the past years. This may indeed be caused by a crucial inconsistency in the proposals: the fact that despite their demand for autonomous development they remain oriented towards the metropolitan countries. As a consequence the satellite countries have hardly concentrated on the implementation of equivalent national policies or the strengthening of horizontal linkages.

This inconsistency is in particular represented by the continued emphasis on the need for North-South transfers of resources, the deceptive notion of 'interdependence' and the 'global' orientation.

The latter is clearly demonstrated by the now almost unanimous acceptance of the significant semantic shift from the 'new *international* information order' to the 'new *world* information order'. Also in the report of the Brandt Commission one finds the thinking about new international relations couched in terms of 'global problems' and 'global solutions'. This 'global' approach is based upon a projected degree of homogeneity, a 'world' model that claims universality in the applicability of scientific and technical progress. Against this, historical reality demonstrates a heterogeneity that makes diverse scientific and technical developments and applications essential.

The 'global' orientation of the new order debate obscures exactly the need of diversity in problem-definition and solution. The 'global' orientation also obscures the inadequate and often regressive national attitudes and policies towards the design of equivalent national and regional restructuring.

As the participants of the Policy Workshop on Communication Research in Third-World Realities (Institute of Social Studies, 1980) stated:

> *The international debate has helped to complicate and sometimes dilute national confrontations on communications policies.*

As a result of the 'global' orientation, 'several Third-World governments have been able to obscure their highly unsatisfactory national arrangements in the area of communications, using their international Third-World position as a political alibi.'

The present NIEO/NIIO debate provides a highly debilitating framework for a constructive approach towards strengthening South-South information networks. It puts insufficient emphasis on the implementation of adequate national infrastructures as prerequisites for such networks.

Perspectives

What, then, can be offered as realistic perspectives: perspectives on the lessening of technological dependence in the south and on the strengthening of technological capacity as an important component of an autonomous development process? Such perspectives would need to give realistic recognition to the fact that present North-South relations in the field of technology prove once again that 'cooperation' and 'interdependence' are inadequate concepts in that they assume 'shared and mutual interests in the common solution of global problems'. The reality of negotiations on such topics as the law of the seas, energy, raw materials, and commodity trade, the unwillingness of the north to cooperate with the south demonstrated at the UNCTAD meetings, the inability to achieve agreement on the 'Group of 77' proposals for equitable participation of the south in international monetary decision-making, show that mutual interests between north and south are an ethical fiction on the part of those who want to inspire international relations with humane considerations.

The scarcity of resources, such as energy and food, is often quoted as the prime motive for mutual dependence and reciprocity in international relations. The response by the US, the most powerful actor in those relations and with the tacit support of most of its allies, has been to cut back on funds for the World Food Programme and to initiate 'rapid deployment forces' to guarantee its free access to the world's common resources.

The notion of global problems (food, energy, health, raw materials) is also misleading. Management of the oceans, for example, is often used as the model of a global problem which needs a global solution. This has an ethical appeal, but is partly incorrect and partly irrelevant. Problems affecting the globe are identified, analyzed and solved to the interests of the most powerful actors.

In technology, in particular, it is abundantly clear that the interests of the chief actors in the north are very different to those of people who seek genuine and autonomous development in the south. Take the example of the United Nations Conference on the Law of the Seas (UNCLOS). Developing countries are strongly in favour of an International Sea-bed Authority (ISA), a supranational body for decision-making on the exploration and exploitation of those parts of the sea bed (outside territorial waters and the exclusive economic zones) which can be considered 'the common heritage of mankind'. To this ISA the necessary technology should be transferred. It is this transfer of technology, however, which has created great resistance on the part of the US delegation. Its spokesmen argue that such transfer would be disadvantageous for the producers of advanced technology. If the US persists, the ISA will not be set up.

Such opposing interests are not easily solved by revisions of patent conventions or by the adoption of codes of conduct. The concentration of knowledge, the exclusive property of technological innovations, and restrictive business practices, are no *ad hoc* arrangements, but are intrinsically related to vital commercial interests and will not surrender to political demands, however morally justified. Neither will they easily give way to such notions as 'enlightened self-interest'. This misleading notion has been highlighted by the Brandt Commission: 'Both north and south have an interest in the effective transfer of capital and technology, which can bring great benefits in terms of expanded production, trade and jobs.' Apart from the fact that it is a totally unrealistic proposition, its basic weakness is that it takes no account of what would happen if present-day 'convergence' technology were to be transferred effectively. Production and trade would be expanded, but only as functions of vertically integrated corporations that are headquartered in the north, and with the end result of the ever firmer incorporation of advanced parts of the south into the present economic order. Jobs, however, would not be increased but would gradually be displaced by automated machinery. By the year 2000, the ILO expects a potential labour force of almost two billion in developing countries. In other words, given current unemployment, an additional one billion jobs will have to be found, 50% of which should be found in agriculture. It might be asked whether this could not be achieved by fundamental land reforms rather than by North-South technology transfer. The remaining 50% would have to be found in industry and in the service sector, precisely where the effective transfer of technology from the north to the south will make labour redundant.

'Enlightened self-interest' offers the perspective of the 'new realism'. This brand of development thinking has become increasingly popular since 1978, particularly in OECD countries. It connects aid to trade and proposes that, with the help of increased aid flows, developing countries will increase their capacity to buy imports. The resultant improved trading relations will be to mutual benefit and in the mutual interest. Aid flows, however, tend to be directed mainly towards the 'middle-income countries' which produce the trading partners who can be integrated into the present international economic order, thus further disintegrating the south.

Self-interest, however 'enlightened', is ultimately nothing but self-interest. Therefore, if, as the Brandt Report claims, 'The North-South discussion on the sharing of technology must continue on many fronts. It is vital to the objectives of a new order', it could be objected that the continuation of the North-South discussion is in fact hindering a new order. A realistic perspective would view North-South technological cooperation as unfit to meet the interests of the south, and would pose as the crucial question. 'How can developing countries mobilize such bargaining power as to negotiate successfully with the north for access to that knowledge which they need in order to develop indigenous capacity to solve their own problems?' Since it is the lack of this bargaining power that has caused such initiatives as the New International Economic Order to fail, emphasis should be placed primarily on the strengthening of national, regional and interregional joint ventures in the south before any grand scheme for international re-ordering is to be attempted.

An obvious starting point for southern strategy would seem to be that technological choices have to be made – consciously and critically – which are in line with defined development objectives. This implies that the appropriateness of any technology chosen for application in the process of development will depend upon its contribution towards those objectives. Appropriateness is not measured in terms of the dimensions of that technology, but as a function of the relation between technology and development. This position leads away from the rather fruitless 'advanced versus appropriate' debate. In meeting specific needs under specific conditions, the combinations of the most complex with the simplest, the largest with the smallest, are possibly the most adequate.

The mixture may not even be 'intermediate', but may blend the 'latest and the best' with 'primitive technology'. In Schumacher's thinking, intermediate technology was seen as vastly superior to primitive technology and at the same time as cheaper, simpler, freer and less violent than the 'supertechnology of the rich'. Development, however, may demand that advanced knowledge be exploited for the upgrading of primitive techniques. It may also invite the application of supertechnology in order to subvert the rich man's use of it. This conception of appropriate technology points to 'technology assessment' as the central activity of acquiring parties which want to select, to integrate and to generate technology. Technology assessment comprises the total process of evaluation, distribution, application and production of technical knowledge/information. Technology assessment is the capacity to process 'technology about technology'. Creating such capacity as a concern of primary importance.

The development of technology assessment capacity needs the transfer of knowledge, not only technical knowledge, but a holistic package encompassing traditional techniques, anthropological, sociological, economic and juridical insights, methodologies of policy analysis, and epistemological tools. Vis-à-vis the transfer of this knowledge, the concept 'appropriate' is definitely 'inappropriate' in that it presents an undue restriction. In constructing capacity for selection, access to the widest possible body of knowledge is an absolute prerequisite. The appropriateness of certain technical information can only be assessed after ample consultation of the largest variety of sources. Once technology assessment capacity has been secured, appropriate technology should become a tautology.

There are currently promising signs of increasing commitment from developing countries to engage in economic and technical cooperation among themselves. Such increased regional and interregional joint ventures can strengthen local capacity for self-reliant development and enhance conditions for collective bargaining power.

During the 1970s the share of Third-World countries' trade among themselves in the total world trade has increased from 3.5% in 1970 to 6.1% in 1979. Whereas between 1955 and 1970 the annual average growth rate of trade flows among Third-World countries was 6.6%, which was well below rates of growth for other trade flows in the world, since 1971 the annual growth rate has been 28%.

There has been a particularly rapid increase in the trade of manufactured products. In 1978 the share of manufactured products in total trade among Third-World countries was 52.7%, which compared with slightly over 25% in 1960 and 42% in 1970. Some manufactured products seem to have a strong potential for substituting for imports from the metropolitan countries. They include products for which Third-World countries have an increasing industrial potential, such as consumer electronics (radio and television receivers), electronic components (transistors) and telecommunication equipment. There are, however, serious obstacles to overcome if this horizontal cooperation is to gain strength. Among the problems are the residual metropolis-satellite links that influence the direction of international trade, especially through preferential schemes offered by the metropolitan market economies and through various strings attached to aid programmes. The deficiencies in transportation and communication infrastructures among the Third-World countries are also impediments. The perennial problems of the balance of payments and of obtaining long-term credits add to the difficulties. Many Third-World countries do not have adequate trade policies to foster cooperation among themselves, and exorbitantly high protectionist charges are imposed on products from other Third-World countries.

Conclusion

The South

The Third World, not yet in the information age but approaching it, should be suspicious of assistance and cooperation from the north. If the Third World is to survive in the information age, its programme for survival will need to be based on the building of a strong, autonomous, information technology infrastructure. Only on such a basis can the bargaining position be created from which the Third World might hope to engage in meaningful technological negotiations with the developed world. At times, this may need the courage to leave the uncomfortable partnership between northern information technology and southern development: a divorce that can only benefit the weakest party.

North-South

Audiences in the north may be left puzzled as to their contribution in the scheme outlined above. For over two decades the emphasis has been on northern assistance to and cooperation with the south. On balance, this has brought more benefit to the north than to the south.

In the development decade that just began assistance and cooperation need to be de-emphasized. It is not that this would not create grave problems, especially for the poorest countries, but only in an ideal world would assistance and cooperation solve the problems they now so abundantly create. In this context technology transfer from north to south is a misleading notion and North-South technological cooperation a deceptive promise. They form a shaky basis for 'a programme for survival'. If the south is to survive in the 'information age' it needs a strong autonomus information technology infrastructure. This it can only acquire if it has the courage to leave the uncomfortable partnership of northern technology and southern development. Their separation can only benefit the weakest party.

The south will thus have to compose its own listing of priorities and the north can only if requested respond to this. More important, however, will be the

major contribution the north could render: to refrain from any interference
– even well intended with developments in the south. As the Cocoyoc
Declaration admonishes scientists in the north: 'Hands off. Leave countries
to find their way. . . refuse to be used for purposes of denying another nation
the right to develop itself.'

The North

The need for a critical and comprehensive technology assessment is as strong
in the north as it is in the south.

The general trend in most of the industrialized countries is to introduce
advanced information technology as rapidly and massively as possible without
coherent, long-term plans for the control of its social consequences.

In acts of sheer social irresponsibility several countries jump on the microelectronics bandwagon with prayer and hope, but without policy. Since the
social cost-benefit analysis is at least unclear in its outcome, the most precious
commodity the north needs now is 'time'. There seems presently neither good
reason for 'Luddite' destruction of information technological applications, nor
good reason for a cheerful 'technological fix'.

There seems, however, good reason for a 'moratorium' or at least a
'temporization' of the further application of advanced information technology, since serious assessment of the social impact of this technology has not
yet started and instruments for the control of deleterious consequences (in
such areas as employment, privacy, centralization of administration) have not
yet been developed.

In Australia the Council on Trade Union Policy proposed in 1979 a five-year
moratorium on new technology in order to study the impact of computerization on society.

Proposals for moratoria or temporizations should not be seen as irrational
attempts to halt 'progress'; they are meant as acts through which we gain time.

Today we need to gain time, exactly because we have so little time left. We
are perilously close to global disaster because of the increasing reliance –
particularly in critical military decisions – on the intelligence of electronic
systems. These systems are characterized by such complexities that their
calculations have become difficult to verify for the human mind.

Human responsibility has not yet been delegated fully to the information
machines. It is still up to us to decide in which world we shall live tomorrow,
unless we let time slip away.

The Microelectronics Revolution: Implications for the Third World

Juan F Rada
International Management Institute, Geneva

Introduction

This paper will attempt to show how the unfolding of information technology affects Third-World countries and poses a challenge to traditional development strategies. It should, however, be seen in a much broader context – the study of how developments in science and technology affect the international division of labour. Today we are faced with microelectronics, tomorrow biotechnology and, on the horizon, the substitution of materials; all three have profound implications for Third-World and industrialized countries alike. These issues will change the very fabric of society and the future of the social, cultural, economic and political life within countries in the international system.

Microelectronics and information technology

The spectacular developments taking place in information technology are posing questions at such a pace that, even before answers can be found, a new wave of even more complicated issues emerge to confront policy- and decision-makers.

The manifold consequences of information technology are explained by at least three interrelated issues: a) its economy; b) the sectors and activities it touches; and c) the concentration of the industrial and R&D capability that pushes it.

Economy

Information is a multifaceted 'commodity' assuming different forms and undergoing continuous metamorphosis through its use and circulation. It constitutes the material base of knowledge, the raw material of news, and an essential component of science, business and trade. Since World War Two, the number of activities dependent on different forms of information has grown exponentially (business decisions, research and development, political matters, legislation, consumption). The number of people dealing with information has also grown.

The presence of a large potential market for information, coupled with the technological 'spill-over' of the United States military and space programmes (e.g. high-performance integrated circuits, satellites, laser technology, etc.), explains the increasing price/performance economy of the information 'package technology', which encompasses components, computers and tele-communications.

By using photographic techniques, 65,000 components are now packed in one 'chip', the size of a little fingernail; in the early 1960s, the density was 10 per 'chip'. With electronic beam and X-ray patterning techniques, the density per chip will increase to a forecast one million components (Very Large Scale Integration – VLSI) with a corresponding reduction of cost per function. The cost reduction resulting from higher integration has been unparalleled. The electronic calculator is a well-known example; its cost has been reduced by a factor of 500:1 in the past eight years, while its performance, reliability and number functions have increased.[1]

Table 1 Comparison of the characteristics of a 1955 computer and a 1978 calculator

Characteristics	1955 Computer (IBM 650)	1978 Calculator (TI-59)
Components	2000 vacuum tubes	166,500 transistor equivalents
Power (KVA)	17.7	0.00018
Volume (cu.ft)	270	0.017
Weight (lbs)	5,650	0.67
Air conditioning (tons)	5 to 10	None
Memory capacity (bits)		
– primary	3,000	7,680
– secondary	100,000	40,000
Execution time (milliseconds)		
– Add	0.75	0.070
– Multiply	20.0	4.0
Price	200,000 ($ 1955)	300 ($ 1978)

Source: Texas Instruments, Inc., Shareholders Meeting Report, 1978.

At the heart of developments are the memory chips, microprocessors and microcomputers which together constitute the 'nuts and bolts' of the information revolution.

Table 1 compares price/performance and the use of other auxiliary systems.

In telecommunications and related equipment, the economy has also been tremendous. A good indicator is the fact that, even taking inflation into account, it cost about 100 times more to call from the United States to London 50 years ago than it does today.[2] The cost of telecommunications is decreasing through the use of satellites since the distance of a communication has virtually no effect on the price.

In 1965, a single satellite carried 240 telephone circuits; today they can carry 12,000. In 1965, the cost per circuit per year was US $22,000; today it is US$800. For 1985, the next generation predict 100,000 circuits at a cost per circuit per year of US$30. The cost of launching satellites will be considerably reduced by the use of the NASA Space Shuttle. At the same time, the cost of ground stations has been falling from about US$10 million in 1965 to about US$300,000 now. Small receive-only ground stations are being sold in Japan for US$200.[3]

Decreasing costs have been accompanied by a tremendous increase in the speed of transmission due to the digitalization of messages. Thus the speed of transmission of the Satellite Business System (IBM and AETNA Casualty Insurance) is 6.3 million bits per second or 200,000 words as compared to nearly 10,000 bits per second for a normal telephone line.

Adding to the cornucopia of developments is the arrival of fibre-optics, which consist of a tube of self-reflecting glass no thicker than a human hair which carries messages in digital form using laser beams. One fibre-optic cable can transmit 30,000 simultaneous telephone calls, as opposed to a package of copper wires 10 inches in diameter. Once certain technical constraints are overcome, fibre-optics will become the standard cable.[4]

The concurrence of components, computer and telecommunications will transform profoundly many human activities.

Areas affected by information technology

The digitalization of different forms of information permits the use of technology in many areas.[5] It is explicitly an organizational and production technology and as such it affects:

1 Production, by the transformation of products (watches, cash registers, etc.) and processes (batch production, robotics, distributed intelligence, etc.).

2 Office work, by further automating formalized work (billing, invoicing, word processing) and by increasing the independence from traditional information channels for those who work in a less formalized environment (management, R&D, etc.)

3 Services, by increasing self-service and by the replacement of human-to-human services by goods.

4 Information flows, due to the economic development of vast networks and easy access to stored information.

The OECD Interfutures report characterized the development of microprocessors as 'a decisive qualitative leap forward' and states:

> *The electronics complex during the next quarter of a century will be the main pole around which the productive structures of the advanced industrial societies will be reorganized.*[6]

The concentration of manufacturing and service capabilities

The nature of information technology and the cost of its development imply that it can only be economically viable when aimed at a world market. In the component, computer, telecommunication, software and machine services, the industry is transnational and highly concentrated. The degree of concentration will most likely increase in the future, due to R&D costs and capital requirements.[7] Underlying this concentration is the integration of many different activities under the heading 'information processing'. Thus computer giants such as IBM have moved into telecommunications (Satellite Business Systems). Office equipment manufacturer Rank Xerox is moving in the same direction, while AT&T is moving into computer terminals and related equipment. Some European PTT and private companies are also moving in this direction and manufacturers of components are shifting to finished products.

US supremacy in the field of integrated circuits has been decreasing due to price competition from Japan. In Japan, Europe and the USA the industry is highly concentrated with few companies controlling more than half of total production. At the same time, some of the biggest producers of integrated circuits do not sell in the open market, such as IBM and Western Electric. There has been a trend in the past few years for setting up captive facilities.[8]

The components' sector is becoming even more capital-intensive than in the past, diminishing the proportion of direct labour cost in the total business cost. This is particularly striking where automation of 'chip' testing and assembly is introduced. The advantages of offshore installations are also being eroded for the same reason.

A similar situation already exists in the computer industry, with only a few companies controlling the business worldwide. At the same time, most of these companies are linked through marketing, technological and manufacturing joint-venture arrangements. This convergence is bound to intensify along with business concentration due to the financial R&D requirements.

The US, Western Europe and Japan possess most of the world computer population, though the dominating force is the US, which controls about 90% of the computer sector in the market economy countries. All major computer manufactures have facilities in several countries and worldwide marketing and service networks.

US manufacturers supply almost 100% of their home market and it is only relatively recently that some inroads have been made by European and Japanese producers, particularly in minicomputers and peripheral equipment. IBM alone supplies about 65% of the US market. Table 2 illustrates the world market share of the major computer manufacturers for mainframe computers.

Table 2 Mainframe computer market* (share of market based on the value of total units installed)

Company	per cent
IBM	64.3
Honeywell	8.7
Sperry Rand-Univac	8.0
Burroughs	6.4
Control Data	4.1
NCR	1.9
Others	6.6

* For details of market shares in Western Europe and Japan, see *Datamation,* September 1976, pp 63 and 93 respectively.

Source: Quantum Science Corporation, 1979.

The revenue of the main US computer companies more than quadrupled from $12.2 billion in 1972 to $53.3 billion in 1980. In 1980 IBM's share of the industry's total revenues was 49%.[9]

The situation is similar in the telecommunications industry, with a few companies controlling and developing electronic switching and related equipment.

A similar concentration exists in software and machine services, data banks and bases. Table 3 shows the concentration in services.

Table 3 Main companies providing software and machine services in 1978 (millions of US dollars)

Software		Machine services	
Computer Sciences (USA)	198	IBM (USA)	400*
System Devt. Corp. (USA)	145	CDC (USA)	400
SOGETI-GEMINI (France)	115	Automatic Data Proc. (USA)	310
Informatics (USA)	85	General Electric (USA)	250
Planning Res. Corp. (USA)	80	EDS (USA)	220
Electronic Data Systems (USA)	70	Tymshare (USA)	150
SEMA (France)	60	Mac-Auto (USA)	130
SCICON (UK)	50	GSI (France)	100
		CISI (France)	95

* Estimate
Source: Pierre Audoin Conceil in Le Sicob, *Le Monde*, 19 September 1979.

In the case of data bases and data base records, Table 4 shows geographic distribution of bases, with about 49% in the US holding nearly 64% of records.

Data banks and bases have their origin in the late 1950s and on-line information searches are growing at a rate of 30% per year. It is not difficult to locate the most important users and 'owners' of the information stored in data banks: 75% of the two million computer searches carried out annually originate in the US. The world's 'big two' data base hosts are Lockheed and SDC (System Development Corporation), which account for 75% of the European market and 60% of the US market. In 1977, Lockheed possessed about 100 of the 500 publicly available data bases in the world.[10] The tremendous concentration of manufacturing and service facilities poses crucial economic, social and political questions that need to be addressed promptly.

The global scope of the information industry is an essential element in understanding its impact. The concentration of financial and technological capital in a few companies and countries will increase dependence rather than interdependence between countries. For some time, this point has caused concern in Western Europe and the Third-World countries, and a number of policies have been designed to counteract the trend.

The impact of information technology

The implications of this powerful technological package which is just unfolding range from the alteration of the productive infrastructure to questions of cultural identity and dependence. The aim here is to restrict the discussion to some general issues directly pertinent to the Third World.

The productive infrastructure

The impact of developments in science and technology on the international division of labour has long been a neglected issue, although innumerable examples exist. Many of them show an erosion of comparative advantages by technological change which, incidentally, shows how endogenous technology is to development.

**Table 4 Reference data bases and data-base records:
geographic distribution, 1975–79**

	Year		
Area	**1975**	**1977**	**1979**
United States			
Number of data bases	177	208	259
Number of records (million)	46	58	94
Other Developed Market Economies			
Number of data bases	124	154	269
Number of records (million)	6	13	55
Total			
Number of data bases	301	362	528
Number of records (million)	52	71	148

Source: Martha E Williams, Data Base and On-line Statistics for 1979, *ASIS Bulletin,* No 7, December 1980, pp 27–29.

What we face today is the concentrated force of two elements: the reorganization of the productive infrastructure based increasingly on technology, which in turn is increasingly dependent on scientific developments. This has been called 'knowledge-based industrial capacity', applying especially to 'high-technology industries, e.g. nuclear, aerospace, computers, etc. It was argued – simplifying the issue here – that while industrialized countries will preserve their lead in these sorts of industry, the Third-World countries will increasingly take over 'labour-intensive industries', since their comparative advantage is low labour costs. Most of the arguments for an NIIO are based on such premises, as was the 'Lima Target' of having 25% of the world industrial capacity in the Third World by the year 2000.

The Third World's capacity in science and technology is a well-debated issue and the world imbalance in this field is too well documented to be repeated. The point now is that most industries are actually in the process of moving towards the 'high-technology' category or can potentially move in that direction due to a combination of socio-economic and technological developments.

Due to the application of microprocessors, microcomputers, alteration of products and process, office automation and other changes, the productivity increase in industrialized countries is at or can potentially reach levels which are competitive with low labour costs.

Automation, by reducing the importance of direct labour cost in total business cost, implies that the incidence of this factor of production diminishes and others, such as capital equipment, design and management, become much more important. At the same time, there is a shift of skill requirements towards software-based and system-engineering skills which are more difficult to attain and develop than those commonly used in basic industries in the past.[11]

The technical and international division of labour is acquiring a new dynamism which calls for a reconceptualization of traditional thinking. The theory of comparative advantages was classically defined by Paul Samuelson when he said that it is 'better for fat men to do the fishing, lean men the hunting, and smart men to make the medicine'. But what happens when the fat men do the fishing, the hunting and make medicine? What happens when electronics becomes a *convergence* industry, indispensable to other industries, conditioning skill requirements and affecting employment levels? What will this mean for development strategy in terms of productive infrastructure? What of the Third World's hopes of acquiring a powerful industrial capability? Even under the most optimistic assumptions, it will not be possible to meet the 'Lima

Target' by the year 2000, without even considering present technological changes and trends.[12]

The industrialized countries have engaged themselves in a far-reaching policy of readjustment provoked largely by competition among themselves, lower growth prospects, high and most likely higher unemployment in the future, higher energy costs, and competition from some Third-World countries. One of the most important tools in this readjustment process is the use of new technologies, particularly microelectronics, for the upgrading of products and processes.

The Advisory Council for Applied Research and Development (UK) summarized the position by stating: 'If we neglect or reject it [semiconductor technology] as a nation, the United Kingdom will join the ranks of the underdeveloped countries.'[13]

Trends in several industries show changes in investment patterns and location of facilities, and industries which were potential candidates to move south will remain in the north.

The electronics industry has traditionally used offshore installations for the assembling and wiring of 'chips'. Now, due to automatic techniques, the industry is developing its new generation of plants in the industrialized countries. The companies see automation as the only way to minimize costs, increase efficiency, maintain employment levels in industrialized countries and be closer to the majority of end-users.

The latest main investments in the field of integrated circuits are in the US, Japan, England, Scotland, Ireland, France and West Germany.[14] Some operations will remain in Third-World countries in order to exploit regional markets or for the assembling and testing of simpler 'chips' where the production volume does not justify automated plants. Additionally, some plants are moving from higher-cost Asian countries (Hong Kong, Taiwan, Republic of Korea and Singapore) to Thailand and The Philippines in an effort to cut costs further. The rate of plant reallocations will depend on the investment policy, amortization and financial constraints of each company. It is clear, however, that the trend is well under way.

Other examples of this trend are textiles and garments, although the tendency is less apparent. The situation here might not be one of withdrawing plants from the Third World, but rather to maintain current production in the north and recuperate terrain in some fields.

The readjustment policies of industrialized countries have greatly encouraged the automation and updating of industry. Automation is seen as the only way of maintaining industry in the north, albeit with reduced employment. At the same time, this process is leading to further industrial concentration through mergers and takeovers and, inevitably, to an uneven distribution of the technology.

The combined effect of automation and electronic-based innovations is reinforcing the transition of industry as a whole towards the 'high-technology' category, strongly oriented towards R&D and software. There will be improvements in the design of products and processes, quality, planning and marketing, already traditional advantages of industrialized countries. In fact, the links between end-producers, machine manufacturers and electronic/computer firms have been multiplied in a joint effort to achieve higher levels of automation.

Looking at these trends, a report by the ILO states: 'The competitiveness of low-labour-cost firms with labour-intensive techniques is continually being eroded by the installation of high-productivity capital-intensive machines in developed and some developing countries.'[15]

Long-term forecasts with a time horizon to the year 2000 suggest that, by that year, textile production will be so capital-intensive that labour-cost differentials will no longer play the decisive role in total product cost that they do today.[16] This forecast was made in 1976, before the massive introduction of microelectronics, and all the evidence suggests that the timing of the change has been drastically reduced.

Nevertheless, erosion of labour-cost advantages in some Third-World countries will take much longer than in others. One study of 20 countries shows that in textiles, the lowest labour cost (Pakistan) was one-thirtieth of the highest (Belgium). However, it should be added that, in this industry, proximity to the main markets and end-users is a considerable advantage because of the incidence of transport costs in the final price.[17]

Protectionist measures, particularly the quota systems, have forced exporters from some Third-World countries to move up-market in order to obtain more value for the same quantity of products, thus forcing their own industry to upgrade and enter a market where their advantage is the lowest. Those countries and territories with the capacity to upgrade successfully will tend to monopolize the exports of Third-World countries by decreasing the competitiveness of others. It is already becoming evident that, in the upper part of the textile and clothing industry and also in new products, competitive edge is now provided by technology and not by labour costs. Over the medium term, this will permeate the industry as a whole.

Given the state of research on these problems, it is not possible to provide a precise time scale or quantification of side effects. What is clear, however, is that this industry will not enjoy the same importance in Third-World countries as in the past, nor will it be a low investment short-cut for employment provision and external revenues. Once technology becomes the industry's competitive edge, it is only a question of time before reallocation of plants starts taking place.

Preliminary evidence shows that similar trends might be under way in the footwear and leather industry. The possibility of combining low labour costs with high technology is also a doubtful alternative, except perhaps where highly sophisticated machine tools are used. In this case, precision engineering can be substituted by parts assembly which may not warrant investment in automation but which may profitably use cheap labour. A candidate might be the watch and clock industry in the lower segment of the market. However, in most cases the alteration of products leads to industrial concentrations and economies of scale rather than deconcentration. A more general obstacle to the low-labour-costs/high-technology solution is that the technologies are controlled by a few transnational companies with worldwide production and marketing policies. In the field of integrated circuits, there is an explicit policy against technology transfer.

The process of transfer of technology is extremely complex since the industry relied very heavily on trade secrets and what has been called 'intangible knowledge'. In addition much of the state of the art of technology is not transferable due to national security regulations. Companies in general try to avoid transferring technology unless they can get technology or market entry in return.

In this industry, as in all advanced technology industries, what is important is to be part of the *innovation process* rather than have access to the technology of a given product. This is because of the short product cycle of products. The only way to have access to the process of technological change is through participation in equity, which is what many European and US corporations have done by taking over innovative companies.

One of the important new developments in the industry are joint R&D programmes particularly in basic research. This is an extension of joint manufacturing or marketing ventures. Joint R&D has been a characteristic of the Japanese industrial strategy but this is being imitated in the US and Europe.[18]

To turn to another aspect of the new technology, microelectronics is software-based and requires a set of skills which are more sophisticated and difficult to obtain than traditional skills of a mechanical nature. Particularly important in this respect is the shift towards the design of production *systems* rather than separate items of machinery; this calls for systems-engineering skills which are only acquired after high-level training and long experience. The distinction between mechanical and electronics engineers is tending to disappear at a time when Third-World countries are reproducing this now obsolete division of skills. Even in industrialized countries, the transition to electronics in formerly mechanical industries, such as watches and office equipment, has shown that the retraining of personnel is almost impossible and involves high cost and risk, especially when dealing with older workers.[19]

The efficient use of software, besides being a highly sophisticated skill, depends on experience gained in solving programming problems and is thus a further contribution to unequal development between industrial market economy countries and Third-World countries, which is likely to be maintained. There may be a few exceptions to this general rule, however, where creation of software may provide some employment.

In the product cycle of software, its initial development represents about 20% of total revenues, the rest being created in the maintenance, which involves a close relationship with end-users and a vast service network. This suggests that software developed for export by Third-World producers will most likely take the form of sub-contracting by the emerging software industry of the industrialized countries, rather than autonomous businesses. It is in these countries that most of the software market lies.

In the two sectors briefly examined, microelectronics will have a significant effect by eroding the advantage of 'cheap labour'. In addition to these trends, the existence of a single information system provides the capacity to transmit blueprints and specifications directly to machinery, concentrating knowledge and skill with the prime contractor rather than duplicating them in an offshore plant.[20] Office automation, on the other hand, permits further increases in the overall business productivity which, in some cases, might be more valuable than shop-floor increases.* We are witnessing the beginning of an important change. Historical evidence shows how developments of this nature can render obsolete 'comparative advantages' and this is particularly true when the driving force of the reorganization of the productive infrastructure is precisely science and technology.

---

* The use of word-processing equipment increases typist productivity by about 100% (new words typed). This does not necessarily mean the same increase in terms of final products.

However, this science and technology has been increasingly controlled by corporate organizations which do not necessarily ensure socially valuable uses of technology or heed its economic disadvantages to the Third-World countries. Furthermore, the technology as such has an inbuilt organizational concept and its design caters for needs, skills and social forms seldom encountered in the Third World.

At the productive level, the claim for an NIEO must be based on the acknowledgement of those tendencies and the likely possibility that the gap between north and south will be even wider in the future.

The use of these technologies in Third-World countries has the effect of decreasing labour creation potential or producing labour displacement. Thus, the reinforcement of the present international division of labour is coupled with internal effects on employment and obviously on the balance of payments.[21]

Nevertheless, in the analysis of benefits and cost, it should be borne in mind that from an employment point of view, the mechanization of agriculture has a dramatic effect on employment, as compared to industrial or service automation. The conditions in most Third-World countries are so different from the advanced ones, particularly in relation to the labour market, that the experience in relation to employment cannot be extrapolated. In addition, in Third-World countries the equipment is more expensive while labour is less costly, which makes automation an option that is not often followed.

The present informatics order

For the Third World, the policy alternatives in the communication field are becoming more complex. While these countries need to emphasize self-reliance and independence, and protect themselves against further domination of their economic, social, cultural and political life, they also need to participate in the international exchange of views, knowledge and, indeed, commodities. This is a difficult, if not impossible, balance, made all the more complex by the changing information infrastructure.

Digitalization of different forms of information creates a tremendous potential increase in productivity, but it also affects the forms and means of information flows.

In the first place, the digitalized network produces a fusion of print, voice and video, blurring the traditional distinction between the different means of communication. All messages are transmitted in indistinguishable strings of ones and zeros; each node in the network, as in the telephone system, can be an originator and receiver of messages in multiple forms. This is no longer a possibility but a reality reflected in services such as teletext (Viewdata or Prestel), integrated office systems and on-line data networks.

In the second place, this fluid network has no frontiers and the insensitivity to distance of broadband bitstreams does not allow national segmentation.

Transborder Data Flows (defined as the transmission of machine-readable information across borders) and the development of interactive international networks is one of today's crucial developments. These networks provide 'real-time' access to information regardless of location. Information can be stored in remote computers and retrieved from many places. Information is, however, an intangible 'good' which is extremely difficult to monitor and which possesses great political, cultural and economic importance. Strings of ones and zeros can be used to transmit documents, voice or image over telephone lines, microwaves and satellites; they can be ciphered and manipulated, and the sheer number of users makes monitoring difficult.[22]

There are two main issues here. The first deals with the type of information being used and the second deals with transborder data flows that will be treated later. The first type of information can be tailor-made, specialized information that can be retrieved through electronic systems without the use of traditional means such as newspapers, radio and the mass media in general. The alternative is the specialization of these traditional means of communications through increasing fragmentation with local and specialized items taking most of the coverage, while editorial, political and international news are beamed to the local press from a central location.

The first alternative is the one most used by business and government, with specialized organizations producing and storing information in central data banks and bases. This is often more influential in determining policy than the traditional media and escapes traditional forms of social control and monitoring.

The second alternative creates the possibility of a more concentrated control of the 'content', with a 'mother-newspaper' dictating the editorial line to many provincial or even foreign newspapers.

The concentration of data banks and bases in the hands of a few companies and countries aggravates the issue. The 'biased' character of international press agencies is well documented, but we now need to consider the 'biased' character of the background information used to produce the analytical news.

Computerized information leads to a different form of exchange and interpretation. Figures and data do not provide for the social context or political realities. Nevertheless, the computerization of references and data leads to a further normalization and quantification of the socio-political analyses. The growth of GNP as a standard of progress, and the balance of payments as a standard of economic soundness, regardless of required structural changes, permeates the technocratic 'bias' of such information systems. The data base entry word for 'democratic movements could easily be 'subversion'. 'Intervention in Third-World countries' could be listed as 'Democracy. . . defence of' and 'Arabian oil' as 'National interest. . . strategic'. The normalization of information does not lead to its 'objectivization'; on the contrary, it leads to an apparent scientificity in the same manner as using an average leads to a figurative representation and to false reproductions of reality.

Interactive information systems should not be opposed to, but rather geared towards, a more balanced and diversified expression of news and realities. As *télématique* progresses, this sort of system will be the *main* source of information for news, education, scientific work and political decisions. The present control, concentration and organization of data banks and bases, and of information technology hardware, not only make the use of these information networks inadequate for the Third World's needs but also reproduce the old patterns of dependency and domination between north and south. The Nora Report, officially endorsed in France, stated:

Information is inseparable from its organization and form of storage. In the long term, it is not only the advantage that the knowledge of one or other piece of data provides. The knowledge will end up by modelling itself – as it always has done – on the stocks of information.

Left to others, e.g. American banks, the task of organizing this 'collective memory', and putting up with delving into it, is equal to accepting cultural alienation. The location of data banks constitutes an imperative of sovereignty.[23]

The second main issue concerns Transborder Data Flows (TDF), which increase the dependency of the Third World due to the concentration of data processing facilities in the industrialized countries. This, in turn, makes the Third World vulnerable to decisions taken in the country holding the data. Third-World countries tend to use the data processing facilities of the industrialized countries for several reasons: routine data processing can be done more economically, the data centres may possess expertise not available locally, and their data bases contain vital information not obtainable in the Third World.[24]

Data flows in the direction of short- and/or long-term economic advantage, and most of this exchange of data relates to intercorporate requirements. The worldwide manufacturing, marketing and financial policies of transnational corporations imply that data providing the bases for decision-making (raw data) flow towards the headquarters and data containing decisions already taken flow towards the subsidiaries (policies).

But this is the tip of the iceberg. What is in fact taking place today is a process of growing information content of goods and services. Traditionally the service sector has been considered the place where most 'information processing' takes place, but this traditional concept is changing due to the 'information intensity' of consumer and capital goods.

Brazil has been one of the first Third-World countries to react to the changing situation. The Executive Secretary of the Special Secretariat for Informatics sees the issue as follows:

TDF, given its fast growth, is an essential component of a more embracing process: the informatization of society. This is the back-cloth to which all of us who operate in the informatics or communication field are submitted. The consequences of this process to nations are not yet known – as neither were the effects of the industrial revolution at the end of the last century. However, there exists a constant aspect: the feeling that the union of telecommunications and informatics will have a strong impact on the culture of the next generation. Some countries have already even established institutional models to prepare their populations, for example Japan and France. TDF as an indicator of this process should have its social effects evaluated. The Brazilian Government intends to etablish a mechanism for this purpose.

He later states:

In international trade a new merchandise has emerged – information – without material consistency and containing its own characteristics, challenging even the basis of western economic policy, property, the right to exclusive use and the competitive set-up. The political frontiers which a short time ago surrounded physical areas and protected the nation's privacy have begun to become scattered.[25]

Brazil has implemented a number of measures to minimize adverse effects to current change while trying to exploit the new opportunities that are open.

The Canadian Minister of State for Science and Technology, opening the Congress of the International Federation of Information Processing in 1977, summarized the issues when he stated:

The problem of transnational data flows has created the potential of growing dependence, rather than interdependence, and with it the danger of loss of legitimate access to vital information and the danger that industrial and social development will largely be governed by the decisions of interest groups residing in another country.[26]

This, of course, is not a hypothetical question; its implications are largely political. The risk of retention or selective release of data is real. Under conditions of economic war, deterioration of the international political climate or, indeed, by unilateral decisions, a country can withhold data with extremely harmful consequences. In the US, the transfer of know-how, software, equipment, etc., can be regulated by the State Department (Jackson Amendment, 1974) and effectively used as a tool in foreign policy. Recent international events show how effectively this can operate, and Third-World countries realize through past experience that this sort of mechanism operates to influence their international economic and political decisions.

The power of those who control data services, hardware, manufacturing, machine and software services increases in direct proportion to the diffusion and widespread use of information technology.

From an economic point of view, the shipping of data to industrialized countries for processing – mostly intracorporate – leads to a loss of jobs or job-creation potential and concentration of capabilities in the information'-rich' countries.

A case in point is Canada, where a government report in 1977 asserted that 7,500 data processing jobs and about $300 million in revenue were being lost because data processing was done abroad. The projections for 1985 estimate losses of 23,000 jobs and $1.5 billion in revenue.[27] This study refers to directly related jobs and was published in 1978. Since then the trend has been confirmed by a recent report submitted to the Canadian Department of Communications. The Canadians suffer severe dominance by foreign capital in their industry and services, and many corporations ship their data abroad for processing. Foreign capital is also dominant in many Third-World countries. This is a growing pattern, curtailing progress in the development of local data processing facilities. The pressure on the balance of payments relates in this case to a service as well as the hardware and infrastructure required to receive the service. For example: France spends about US$2.5 million a year consulting US-based data banks and data bases.[28]

Furthermore, due to the decreasing cost of communications and the concentration of 'information-intensive' sectors in industrialized countries, it is becoming cheaper in many cases for Third-World enterprises and institutions to send their design problems, calculations, research and routine data abroad rather than to assemble and develop local teams. What happens, in fact, is a sort of 'electronic brain drain' produced by reducing the opportunities for local development. The ever-growing dependency of many countries on large data networks will increase the importance of these issues.

Of particular importance in the overall question of TDF, besides the issues already mentioned, are those relating to the protection of privacy and cultural identity. The use of vast pools of information to monitor individuals and store information about them is not only real, but has already prompted legislation in several countries and many studies by international organizations. Privacy is a fundamental human right and the necessary legislative tools need to be devised and international standards established to ensure that this right is respected.[29]

Those who today have the leading edge and benefit most from TDF are using the argument of 'free flow' of data as it is used for the 'free flow' of information and commodities. Nevertheless, the unrestricted flow of data needs to be qualified because of potential negative consequences. When dealing with TDF, one encounters a reality that affects in a very concrete form the economic, social, political and cultural life of countries and people.

A 'free and balanced flow of information' – to use the jargon of the trade – is indispensable not only to the Third World but also to most Western European countries.

This debate is encompassing more areas due to the possibilities of direct television broadcasting via satellite, where transmission is beamed directly to individual receivers. There is as yet no test case to evaluate the concrete implications and consequences, and its realization would involve complex and unique technical undertakings. The application is limited at the moment to domestic systems using a common receiving station and passing the message through cable to individual television sets.

70

From a legal point of view, the question was apparently settled by Regulation No 428A of the International Telecommunication Union in 1971, which stipulates that all technical means should be used to reduce the radiation of the satellite beam over the territory of other countries 'unless agreement has previously been reached with such countries'. Nevertheless, the United States, for instance, regards the regulation as a purely technical requirement, having no bearing on the content of transmissions. Furthermore, it would like to consider itself free to take advantage of the potential of satellites, if necessary, without the consent of the recipient country.

Because of the US insistence on the principle of unrestricted free flow, the United Nations Outer Space Committee has been unable to reach agreement on whether the prior consent of the recipient country is required for direct satellite transmission to take place.[30]

It is self-evident that the power of protocols and agreements 'in principle' is minimized when the time comes to voluntarily renounce a commercial, cultural and, indeed, powerful political weapon. This calls for closer attention and monitoring of developments by the Third World. For the time being, the unique technical complexities of this type of transmission make their materialization unlikely in the medium term, but it is one area where anticipatory policy is required in order to be prepared to handle such developments when they reach maturity.

Information technology and development

Information technology poses a formidable challenge to development policy. There are three main reasons for this:

1 Production factors are increasingly conditioned by scientific and technological change, i.e. the industrial and service infrastructure is becoming independent from geographical location, natural or traditional economic advantages.

2 Concentration of the manufacturing and service capabilities of information technology in a few companies and countries makes the danger of growing dependency greater due to the all-pervasive character of the technology and the fact that electronics is becoming a convergence industry.

3 The concentration of 'information-intensive' sectors in industrialized countries and the increase in productivity of commercial and economic transactions further reinforces the traditional advantages of these countries.

Information technology is a reality, and a rapidly expanding one. The question, therefore, is how to master the changes and deal with these issues to the best advantage for development strategies.

What is needed is a socio-economic command of the development of science and technology. It is obvious that the issues being confronted today, which will increase in complexity in the future, demand a global approach. This is also true for science and technology (S&T).

The implementation of such an approach will undoubtedly take many years, but it is unavoidable. In the economic, social and cultural fields, a number of regulations exist, and established mechanisms feed back social concerns; in the future, S&T must also be governed by such mechanisms, as it is becoming increasingly important for every aspect of human activity.

Policy- and decision-makers in the Third World could accelerate this process by putting it on the international agenda. Nevertheless, the process should start within the Third-World countries themselves. The need is to define areas of particular S&T concern, national priorities for their immediate and future needs, and a well-defined timetable of concrete action. This could serve as a starting point for joint efforts at the sub-regional, regional and continental levels and as the basis for proposing programmes and exchanges to the industrialized countries in areas where collaboration could be most fruitful. These steps could be building blocks for a global S&T strategy. The World Conservation Strategy is an example of such a global effort.[31]

Unless Third-World countries – through their existing political tools – start moving in the direction described, they will not have much hope of establishing a New International Order but will rather be reinforcing the present one.

The essential starting point is the development of a system of scientific and technological assessment, forecasting and policy design. There is no time to waste, as changes are already under way with the increasing economy of devices such as robots, the possibility of complex direct verbal input, direct satellite links, etc. In addition, the first significant investments are paying off in biotechnology, which has been called 'the living micro revolution', and considerable research and investment is taking place in areas such as composites for the substitution of metals.

Just as microelectronics is related to the mastering of intelligence functions, the development of biotechnology would seem to be related to the mastering of biological cycles and mechanisms. This will, of course, have a considerable impact on industrialized as well as Third-World countries. Furthermore, information technology increases enormously S&T and R&D capacity by providing easy access to information and interactive relations. This in itself could accelerate the rate of discoveries and innovations.

The Third World can no longer remain a passive observer of changes that were foreseen, digested and transformed into policy in the industrialized countries before the south took notice of their existence and impact at the proper level. The Third World requires a formalized or *ad hoc* instrumentality to assess the types of change described in this article, and also to monitor closely and forecast developments such as substitution of materials and biotechnology.

The capacity for prospective assessment permits not only a better bargaining position, but also puts the elaboration of development strategies on a more solid basis by developing a more refined conceptualization of short-, medium- and long-term comparative advantages.

We must learn how to harness current changes, while avoiding the undesirable effects of technology. In fact, microelectronics-based innovations can be of great benefit if properly applied.

Three general principles apply to the use of technology within countries. First is the need for a national policy based on the selectivity of applications aimed at overcoming bottlenecks and optimizing the use of resources, rather than using the technology to replace labour or increase efficiency which could be increased by other means. This undoubtedly calls for policies that strike a careful balance between pros and cons.

Selectivity and conscious planning can, for instance, minimize hard currency expenditure if data banks and bases are developed for domestic use and export. By avoiding imports of services, the foreign exchange savings could be greater in the medium term than the cost of installing the equipment, while at the same time developing local expertise and capabilities. It will also have the added advantage of organizing a system which meets the needs and culture of the country. Selectivity can also gear applications to areas where it is beneficial for the country as a whole to maintain international competitiveness.

Additionally, selectivity implies a policy on technical obsolescence and upgrading of equipment, together with clear technical criteria on the types of equipment that should be used. This, of course, applies differently to each sector and area. More often than not, equipment is upgraded according to new technical breakthroughs rather than based on a careful evaluation of the alternatives. Old equipment can often be useful and economical, within the objectives of a development plan; there is no need to replace old equipment each time a new product arrives on the international market.

Second is the need to ensure diversified sources of supply in the market and to avoid becoming dependent on a few companies which can greatly distort prices and application criteria because of their disproportionate marketing power. This must be accompanied by a policy on software. The reservation of market segments for nationally or regionally assembled equipment is also an important consideration here. The diversification of suppliers benefits the economy by encouraging price/service performance of producers or importers, thus minimizing their margins and the outflow of profits.

On the service side, the 'technological package' should be unwrapped in such a way that conversion software and other services could be produced locally, providing that an adequate manpower policy is followed to train and develop local personnel and firms.

The diversification of suppliers is the only way to minimize dependency, given the fact that it is highly unlikely that Third-World countries could develop their own manufacturing capabilities. The possibility of manufacturing exists only when the adopted criteria of obsolescence differ from the international market and the system is developed behind strong protective barriers. The technical specifications of the equipment would, however, be several years and generations behind the leading producers. Under these conditions, the manufacturing alternative is only justifiable within a large potential internal market (e.g. India) or within a regional market that could permit appropriate economies of scale.

The difficulties that European manufacturers are encountering when trying to jump on the integrated circuits bandwagon show that the possibilities for Third-World countries are practically nil, especially because in this area, as well as in computers, there is an explicit policy of no transfer of technology. The United States and Japan are so far down the semiconductor industry's learning curve that it might be impossible for European newcomers to catch up, let alone for the Third World.

Third is the need to monitor the national integration of locally assembled or partly manufactured electronic-based products. This is important because, due to technological change, the picture is distorted. In general, countries use an index of national integration combining weight/volume/value to measure how much of a given product is nationally made in compliance, in some cases, with local legislation or plans.

Today, integrated circuits which are the heart of electronic-based products have a very low weight/volume/value, but they incorporate all the 'real' value of the product from the point of view of technology and know-how. If the purpose of a country is to upgrade slowly its own national capability in this area, it is important to monitor national integration in the light of current change. This is also related to the fact that many 'intelligent' products appear under traditional or very general descriptions of import classifications or the SITC (Standards International Trade Classification), which not only could decrease the capacity of local industry to compete, but also implies that many products escape general guidelines and automation policy. For example, in one Latin-American country where a regulatory policy and supporting legislation exist for data processing, it is 'technically' feasible to exclude word processing from the policy and leave it unregulated.

Given the trends described, it is advisable to devise wider information policies rather than computer policies on their own, although, as has been explained, the computer is penetrating all areas and many products.

In order to be more explicit concerning the beneficial use of the technology in the immediate future, certain areas need to be examined. The benefits are related, as mentioned earlier, to the capacity to implement national policies which can balance pros and cons to the advantage of the population as a whole.

Possible economies

The decreasing cost of the technology, as mentioned earlier, in itself permits more economical applications. Nevertheless, the cost of labour in most Third-World countries means that equipment is less competitive and amortization takes longer. Therefore, many traditional technologies and organizational forms will remain competitive for a long time.

In many cases, the use of information technology in products or processes saves capital per unit of output although it increases capital per worker employed. As the saving of capital is a crucial factor for the Third World, the technology could be used beneficially, providing that the application complies with a well-thought-out plan aimed at fulfilling the needs of the majority of the population.

In addition, the use of the technology can be skill-saving in many cases in areas where the development of local skills would be a costly long-term venture; thus, a form of leapfrogging can take place. This is particularly true in the case of precision engineering, where reliable, sophisticated and economical machine tools are becoming available in which most of the skills required are in-built in the programme of the machines. At the same time, traditional equipment is rapidly being pushed to obsolescence, not because it is intrinsically outdated, but because industrialized countries need to use the latest equipment available to be able to compete among themselves. This 'obsolete' equipment can become available at scrap value and remain economically viable when combined with lower labour costs, appropriate skills, and managerial and government policies.

In many of these new areas of development, some skills are not difficult to obtain (conversion software, simple programming, etc), although mastering the programming needs of standard types of equipment is not equal to the creation of innovative capacity and systems-engineering skills. It is one thing to learn how to drive an automobile or a tractor and another to know how to make, repair or upgrade it.

The 'core' of the software is generally part of the producer's package and, as the competitive edge will be increasingly on the software rather than the hardware content, we are witnessing a shift whereby the 'incorporated technology' will become even more important while becoming intangible. 'Reverse engineering' in this context will be even more difficult. It was not at random that many powerful companies, instead of manufacturing their own self-contained systems in the computer field, opted for producing IBM plug-compatible equipment, which uses IBM software, due to the sophistication, cost and service infrastructure required to implement complete software packages.

Transfer of technology, patents and licensing will therefore be much more complex inasmuch as one is dealing with a good as intangible as non-materialized knowledge. At the same time, one needs to bear in mind that current changes are accompanied by increasing concentration, vertical/forward integration, and global marketing production policies.

The technology also carries with it certain diseconomies. Forecast losses because of inadequate use of computerized equipment or losses due to equipment failure could run extremely high. The growing dependency on automatic equipment and the rigidity introduced because of it call for careful evaluation of its use and convenience.

Social and government applications

Computer technology has long been used by government services in Third-World countries, especially for statistical purposes. This could increase further, improving the accuracy, reliability and timing of statistical information valuable for decision-making and planning. The time lag between events/policy implementation and its proper evaluation can be shortened considerably, thus increasing the efficiency of decisions, policy design and the monitoring of the performance of different measures. With a solid information base, the technology can be used to optimize the allocation and use of resources, which in itself could mean considerable economies. A tighter control of commercial stocks, imports and exports, and tax collection could be of great benefit, while saving foreign exchange in many areas.

Although employment could increase marginally when new or supplementary services are created, in general the technology will diminish job-creation potential. Thus a careful evelution is needed to combine traditional and modern methods between desirable information and employment results.

Countries can further their planning and bargaining capacity if they are capable of assembling the relevant information.

Other important areas of application are those which enhance social services, particularly health and education. One of the most beneficial applications of information technology is in health, particularly as aid for the handicapped, prevention of accidents, industrial safety and pollution control, which serve to solve important problems without increasing the 'capital intensity' of the health sector.[32] It must be borne in mind, however, that there is a danger in using the information processing capabilities of computers in the health, banking and social control areas. Computers can communicate in an inter-active network and therefore an insurance company or bank computer can, if arranged, interrogate a health data bank computer concerning the health of a particular client seeking a policy, credit or mortgage. Third-World countries have been slow in enforcing privacy laws and the right of individuals to have access to information stored about themselves, which might be incorrect, incomplete, out of context, or related to events which have already been corrected. This is important at national and international levels, since the technology can be and has already been used for massive violations of human rights.

In education, information technology can serve to enhance economically the capability of the traditional system, integrating remote and isolated sectors with national life and increasing the diversity and national content of programmes. For instance, the economy of audiovisual equipment and production can boost national programmes for schools, television, village education and rural extension, as the mimeograph boosted the local press and atomized the production of educational materials. This could help to avoid the alienating tyranny of imported canned programmes which are foreign to local culture.

However, this potential needs to be qualified. Information technology is accompanied by its own sub-culture and an apparently neutral concept of efficiency and organizational forms, a universal technical language and a functional language: English. Most data banks, bases, keyboards, instructions, literature, etc., related to the technology are in English. This means that only those with an adequate knowledge of the language can have access to many services. There is a tremendous need here for cultural diversity not only linguistically, but also in terms of content and format. Third-World countries should collectively implement the storage of the 'collective memory' in their own language and according to their own interests. How much information is stored and easily available on appropriate technology and the different alternatives to a given production process? How much is stored on traditional medicines and organizational experiences of rural extension programmes? Will a Latin-American country be forced to go to a computer in the US – importing a service – to find out import-export possibilities to India or Nigeria? Will the Third-World newspaper industry be forced – as with the news agencies – to rely for information on data banks and bases in the industrialized countries?

International dimensions

There are many areas where Third-World countries are called upon to act collectively. These could be facilitated by the use of information technology.

Five broad areas were initially identified by the 1975 Dag Hammarskjöld Report *What Now: Another Development,* prepared on the occasion of the Seventh Session of the United Nations General Assembly and put forward as the minimum practicable steps towards Third-World collective self-reliance.[3]

First is the 'coordination of industrial and agricultural development'. The technology can be invaluable here to monitor policies, plan and allocate resources. At the same time, the simple fluid exchange of information could allow massive horizontal links in the field of trade. The lack of marketing capacity of individual countries can be lessened by information networks where country A will know what is available in country B, rather than relying exclusively on the marketing and information drive of companies in industrialized countries and their battery of advertising aids. The development of these types of information network is an important step towards increasing collective self-reliance.

The first step will be for countries to compile such information under generally agreed rules. The information should then be assembled regionally, and finally globally, using the codification of the SITC (Standard International Trade Classification) as an initial guideline. Additionally, joint or coordinated efforts can be facilitated in areas as diverse as transport, marketing consultancy, managerial practices and expertise, and so on.

The second and third areas referred to in the above-mentioned report relate to the development of an autonomous financial capacity and monetary system. This is, of course, closely linked to the first area; it is also heavily conditioned by information exchanges and data processing. The increased productivity of commercial transactions could benefit Third-World countries if used by their own institutions.

The fourth area is the 'strengthening of technological capacities'. This point was largely covered earlier. Diversified and efficient technologies offering flexibility of scale, resource utilization, labour-based product mix and participation already exist in many places, as for example with energy generating/saving devices. The use of fluid information could serve to identify this base and develop channels to make it readily and economically available.

This aspect is closely linked to the fifth area: 'Towards Third-World Communication'. Although the report refers essentially to the questions of news agencies and the need for a different 'Information Order', changes in technology make this much wider. In effect, the whole information infrastructure is suffering profound changes. If the Third World does not develop its own data banks, bases and networks, information relevant to research, science or the mass media will be further concentrated and the system will suffer even more acute problems and disparities than those it faces today. At least two elements are of importance here: the question of cultural identity and diversity mentioned earlier, especially in relation to language, and the classification, codification and sorting systems of present banks and bases. Newspapers (such as the *New York Times*) organize their news banks according to their own editorial line, principles and the characteristics of the news the paper carries, and based largely on their own past news and files. What appears relevant to Third-World countries, in terms of items or content, is not necessarily represented and, furthermore, the analysis will not necessarily conform with the development policies and priorities of the Thrid World. There is no need to underscore here the shortcomings of these systems in the light of the long debate about the New International Information Order.

The issues involved here also concern industrialized countries, for basically the same reasons. Alain Minc stated the point of view of France in an OECD meeting in September 1978.[34]

Unless action is taken, the Third World will buy not only the news but also the background information to produce it and the 'news about the news', ranging from abstracts of magazine articles to book reviews.

Finally, in summary, collective action should be taken in four main areas:

1 Joint efforts to develop technological and scientific assessment and forecasting in those areas likely to affect most profoundly Third-World countries and the international division of labour. Social command of scientific and technological development is thus broader than mere control; it assumes an orientation of S&T development rather than a regulatory and reactive position with regard to changes. This, of necessity, requires a formalized body responsible for assessment and policy recommendations. Its task should be short-, medium- and long-term assessment and policy recommendations as a service to Third-World countries for planning and negotiation purposes.

2 Joint efforts to evolve a common information policy, based on a development of building blocks that could stem from the assessment provided by the body or networks of institutions described above. This policy should encompass data banks, bases, networks in the economic, S&T, R&D, cultural and mass media fields. The Third World should also evolve a common policy towards communications, transborder data flows, satellite links and transfer of technology. Particularly important in this field is to work towards an international agreement to deregulate as much as possible software copyrights, especially in products. It could also evolve into common facilities for manufacturing in selected areas, applications and R&D, with special emphasis, at least initially, on software.

3 Common policies on regulatory international protocols about privacy, monitoring of flows of data, and on information requirements about the type of data that any given institution should hold in a country and/or ship abroad. This is an area where much progress has been made among OECD countries, but the Third World has not participated actively in the debate.

4 Joint efforts to obtain preferential treatment for access to data banks and bases as a way to mitigate the growing gap between north and south in areas such as S&T. Free access to these sources could be part aid and transfer of technology agreements.

At this stage, a warning is necessary: the potential benefits of the technology, as with other technologies, could remain paper and words, as they have in many cases. The benefits assume a short- and long-term direction, i.e. the active search for alternative development strategies. This in the final analysis is related to the power structure within and between countries. If this structure is not altered in most countries and internationally, there is little hope that desirable benefits will materialize.

Data, information and a new productive infrastructure should benefit not only the few; we cannot have a world divided between information-'poor' and -'rich'. Data and information should not be used to infringe on a people's cultural identity and invade, by means of different life styles, patterns of consumption and values, a world that is struggling to reach its own identity and development path. More than legislation and protocols, a new atmosphere of social command of technologies should be developed. In this atmosphere a participatory and plural discussion about the use of technologies could take place and the wonders of current change could help solve pressing needs and benefit all in a more interdependent rather than dependent world.

Information is a 'social good', embodying in its content and form of transmission cultural patterns, social organizations, complex and subtle forms of social reproduction and economic value.

We are confronting a change, as profound as major changes in the past, which masters an essential component of economic activity and human interaction. The outcome of this change will depend on society's ability to harness the technological cornucopia which is unfolding, in order to avoid the creation of an order which might take decades to dismantle. Present change could lead to planetary uniformization and greater dependency for the Third World or it could serve to manifest the basic unity of humanity in the diversity of its expression.

References

1 These points have been developed in greater detail in J Rada, *The Impact of Microelectronics: A Tentative Appraisal of Information Technology*, ILO, Geneva, 1980. See also R Ide, *Microelectronics – The Technological Thrust*, Information & Communications Technology, Ontario, Canada, 1979.
2 R L Merrit, 'The Revolution in Communications Technology and the Transformation of the International System' in C Mendes, *(et al.)*, *The Control of Technocracy*, Brazil, 1979.
3 R Ide, *op.cit.* See also L M Branscomb, 'Computer Technology and the Evolution of World Communications in International Telecommunication Union (ITU)', *Third World Telecommunication Forum*, Geneva, 1979, Part 1.
4 For details on the economy and applications of fibre-optics see K Y Chang, 'Fiber Optic Integrated Distribution and its Applications' in *International Conference on Communications, Conference Record Vol 1*, Boston, MA, June 1979, and K G

Corfield, 'Optical Fibres in Communications – A Re view of the Benefits in ITU', *Third World Telecommunication Forum, op.cit.*

5 For details, see J Rada, *op.cit.*, and G Friedrichs, *Microelectronics: A New Dimension of Technological Change and Automation,* Vienna Centre Conference on Microelectronics, September 1979. Important material is compiled in a pedagogical form in National Extension College, *The Silicon Factor,* London, 1979.

6 OECD Interfutures, *op.cit.*, pp 114 and 336.

7 Most US semiconductor manufacturers (the 'pioneers') have been acquired either wholly or in part by large US and European corporations. In Europe, a process of concentration is also taking place through mergers, takeovers and joint ventures. The EEC Commission has devised a plan to streamline the European electronics industry. Also see J Rada, 'Structure and behaviour of the international semiconductor industry', UNCTC, New York (Forthcoming 1982).

8 J M Fabre and T Moulonguat, 'L'Industrie Informatique' in S Nora and A Minc, *L'Informatisation de la Société,* Vol II, Annexe No 7, Paris 1978; J Rada, Structure and behaviour. . .', *op.cit.*

9 International Data Corporation in *Fortune Magazine,* 5 June 1978, and *Financial Times,* 6 February 1979.

10 *New Scientist,* 11 January 1979. See also 'La guerre des données', *Le Monde Diplomatique,* November 1979. R Beca, 'Les Banques des Données' in S Nora and A Minc, *op.cit.*, Vol I, Annexe No 2.

11 See on this point J Jacobson, *Technical Change, Employment and Technological Dependency,* Research Policy Institute, University of Lund, Discussion Paper No 122, August 1979, and J Rada, *op.cit.*

12 See the outcome of 'Scenario A' in the OECD Interfutures Report, *op.cit.* This is the best possible scenario and the Lima Target is not accomplished, even though the exercise does not consider the technological changes described here.

13 Advisory Council for Applied Research and Development, *The Application of Semiconductor Technology,* London, 1978, p 7.

14 This is the case of Inmos, GEC-Fairchild and ITT in the UK, Thomson-Motorola in France, Mostek in Ireland, National Semiconductors, Motorola and NEC in Scotland and Hitachi in West Germany. See H F L Roessle, 'Prospects for the European Semiconductor Industry' in *Financial Times Conference: Tomorrow in World Electronics,* Conference Papers, London, 1979.

15 ILO, *Programme of Industrial Activities – Textiles Committee,* Geneva, 1978. Report III, p 43.

16 W Hardt, *Die Textilindustrie im Jahr 2000.* International Wool Conference, Basel, 8–12 June 1976, mimeo, quoted in ILO, *Programme of Industrial Activities, op.cit.*, Report II, p 9.

17 Economist Intelligence Unit, *World Textile Trade and Production,* EIU Special Report No 63, London, 1979, p 37.

18 J Rada, 'Structure and behaviour. . .' *op.cit.*

19 See, for instance, B Lamborghini, *The Diffusion of Microelectronics in Industrial Companies,* Vienna Centre Conference on Microelectronics, September 1979.

20 For details on the type of applications, see B Colding, *et al, Delphi Forecast of Manufacturing Technology,* London, 1979, pp 23–25.

21 For details on this point, see J Rada, 'The impact of. . .', *op.cit.,* particularly Chapter 7.

22 Numerous studies exist on this point. Particularly important are two OECD Series: OECD *Informatics Studies* and OECD *Information, Computer, Communication Policy* (ICCP).

23 S Nora and A Minc, *op.cit.,* p 72.

24 J M Carrol, *The Problem of Transnational Data Flow,* OECD Informatics Studies No 10, Paris, 1974, p 203.

25 *Transnational Data Report,* Vol IV No 7, North-Holland Publishing Co., 1981.

26 Quoted by H P Gassmann, 'New International Policy Implications of the Rapid Growth of Transborder Data Flows' in OECD Information, Computer, Communications Policy No 1, *Transborder Data Flows and the Protection of Privacy,* Paris, 1979.

27 *Datamation,* 1 November 1978, p 67. See also *Transnational Data Report,* Vol IV No 6, North-Holland Publishing Co., 1981.

28 *Le Monde Diplomatique,* November 1979, *op.cit.*

29 OECD, *Transborder Data Flows and the Protection of Privacy, op. cit.*

30 The text of the ITU resolution adopted in the Space Conference of 1971 in Geneva is the following: 'In devising the characteristics of a space station in the broadcasting-satellite service, all technical means available shall be used to reduce, to the maximum extent practicable, the radiation over the territory of other countries unless an agreement has been previously reached with such countries.' International Telecommunication Union, *Radio Regulations,* Edition of 1976 revised in 1979, Geneva, 1979, Vol 1. See also N McLeod, 'TV Culture Invasion from Space', *New Scientist,* 28 February 1980, p 645.

31 International Union for the Conservation of Nature and Natural Resources (IUCN), with the cooperation of United Nations Environment Programme (UNEP), World Wildlife Fund (WWF), FAO and UNESCO, *World Conservation Strategy: Living Resource Conservation for Sustainable Development,* Switzerland, 1980.

32 In relation to the 'content' of health systems and services in Third-World and industrialized countries, see *Development Dialogue,* 1978:1, *Another Development in Health,* Uppsala, 1978.

33 *What Now: Another Development,* Dag Hammarskjöld Foundation, Uppsala, 1975, pp 78–84.

34 A Minc, *The Informatization of Society* in OECD Information, Computer, Communications Policy No 3, *Policy Implications of Data Network Developments in the OECD Area,* Paris, 1980, pp 155–156.

Microelectronics, Innovations and New International Information Order

Enrique González Manet
Communication Adviser
Ministry of Foreign Relations, Cuba

Technological and socio-economic change endangers every country's future, developed or underdeveloped alike. Within the coming years we will witness new social issues neither Orwell nor Huxley ever dreamed of. One crucial point is that those which promote, shape and intend to control these forces know not what will be the outcome of such processes. Actual impact of applied science is in itself a clarifying element.

Trends will be irregular and unpredictable. Reality is no more an indisputable fixed reference. It is becoming extremely diversified under a myriad possibilities, interconnections and variables almost impossible to match even through computer simulation.

A basic question is that given values or *status quo* are already being tremendously affected by the introduction of new technological patterns in production and social relations. Whether these forces are intended for the sake of socio-economic control or humanistic solidarity, is yet to be established. But we should recognize that the growing presence of very specific signs indicate that we must prepare ourselves for the worst.

This is not, in any sense, a deliberately pessimistic view of the present situation. Since five years ago – when computer chips began to be mass-produced – we have come to acknowledge that there is a rationalizing, integrating and decentralizing effect on microelectronics, and that one of the most important of its consequences is a devastating impact upon labour.

Public opinion, mostly in Western European countries, is just awakening to the meaning of computer chips and the significance they will have in everyday life, being able as they are to be applied to every kind of logical sequence, from door opening and automatic design to sophisticated weapons development and immediate decision-taking at state level.

Transnational power centres have systematically integrated and moreover disguised these processes and facts through every conceivable channel of message circulation with the purpose of demobilizing political and social action. This confrontation is what we are summoned to deal with.

Have we really thought of the whole range of implications these forces will impose upon mankind? We are in front of a new total control system already being structured and implemented. Most countries in the Third World do not realize what's happening.[1] An exception is the monopolistic power centre whose very aim is the modernization of capitalist structures and the forging of new ways of domination through the management of a wired world based on private satellite interconnected data banks.

Steps in this direction, accelerated by interimperialistic competitiveness, will modify long-established rules, giving way to a radical turnover in social, cultural, economic and political patterns on a global scale.

This does not mean that any technology has such a leading role or overriding influence that it could even neutralize or eliminate social class struggle. On the contrary, they are already deepening it. The question is that changes which can affect production, productivity and manpower levels will also have – and indeed are having – decisive influence on international division of labour and structural relations. In this sense, generalized technological change affects the way people relate, live and behave.

The question is approached from a totally different point of view by American policy-makers, who in the *American Agenda for a New World Order of Communication,* organized and promoted by the US National Commission for UNESCO, openly mention that the way the electromagnetic spectrum and the building blocks of communication will be allocated among all nations will affect the way which we live our lives and run our commerce and industry. This agenda remarks that communications and information systems and technologies are at the lending edge of social, economic, political and scientific developments in the world today, and that a grent emphasis should be placed on encouraging global free flow of information.[2]

Articulated international pressures in this direction have come from countries allied to transnational corporations and State Department's strategy, and non-governmental organizations like the World Press Freedom Committee, Freedom House, American Editors Association, International Press Institute, International Institute of Communication, International Federation of Journalists, Inter-American Broadcasting Association, Inter-American Press Society and the Asian Press Foundation, besides transnational news agencies like AP, UPI, Reuters, France Press and Visnews-UPITN.

In a forthcoming book on the New International Information Order, Kaarle Nordenstreng, president of OIJ, indicates the fact that this pressure against the movement towards a New Order was not only generated in the United States, but had a wider western basis, and is demonstrated by an article on *Freedom of the Press and the Threat of State Intervention,* published in late 1981 in *NATO Review.* In this text, Douglas Hurd, the British Minister of State at the Foreign and Commonwealth Office in London, warns the members of NATO that they must recognize the seriousness of the menace and act together to meet it.[3]

Unable to cope with developing social conscience at world level, to meet urgent demands from backward countries, to counteract issues like those summoned by the Movement of Non-Aligned Countries or to neutralize unrest in Central America, the United States refuses to lower its privileged high standards of living, based on indiscriminate exploitation.

Instead, with the help of microelectronic innovation, the US seeks to impose and extend domination through every conceivable way, at any costs, driving humanity to a demented armamentism career and – something everyone should try to stop – a horrible war that will spare no life on earth.

Actual technocratic tendencies of change within production relations leads the US to militarization of the economy and a fascist orientation of political processes. Signs of these trends are the progressive privatization of the public sector and the freezing of monopolistic capitalism of state, actually forced by Reagan's Administration, which strides wildly to the implementation of a nearly total deregulation policy.

A basic point is that in most cases technology is a specific outcome, a blueprint designed for a given social system and suited to fit concrete financial and economical frames. Informatics, in accordance with profit maximization, could be considered as an instrument to not only improve production but also to streamline the labour force and neutralize labour unions as functional regulatory elements of social equilibrium.

Automation tendencies in industrial and service sectors indicate an increasing rate of unemployment along with negative social costs as direct side effects. These processes, as confirmed by several important reports, official and non-governmental, develop a strong trend in concentrating decisions and at the same time stimulate a generalized decentralization at operational level. This particular consequence has the most important meaning because it makes distance irrelevant to such activities as management, servicing and supervising controls.[4]

In this direction we can find some of the clues to the financial and urban crisis affecting New York; to the swift and carefully controlled build-up of Atlanta, Georgia, as the new financial and communication centre of the United States; and also to the strategical value assumed by 'tax-free paradises', such as the Virgin and Cayman Islands, Jamaica, St Lucia, the Bahamas and Barbados.

We could extend the meaning of these changes to other fields and situations, knowing that amongst different central characteristics of the informatization process – expressing the marriage of computer, laser, tv and satellite technology – we can clearly identify the diversification of multiscctorial investment, financial superconcentration, transnational capitalist expansion and the development of the horizontal and vertical linking of economic structures.

There is a close interconnection between informaties and the New International Information Order. The question is not only that rentability of technology needs global scope, convenient scale operations and unrestricted transborder data flow backed by the acceptance of the 'free-flow' and 'free-access' doctrines.

Informatics is actually being developed as the proper 'new order' needed by huge private transnational corporations to pursue hegemonic domination through new forms of neocolonization. This approach is related to long-range strategies which also include western developed countries as prime targets. It is by no means possible to deny that American monopolist enterprises control 90% in this field.[5]

Western European countries are growingly worried because they only share 6% in the production of electronic components while a single country concentrates 82%, as OECD expert Eric Meyer has mentioned. Besides, the United States operates the six biggest transnational informatics networks and plans a giant multisatellite station for 1985 with the help of the shuttle *Columbia*, apart from its military and strategic missions.

Power centres like Exxon (first in oil) have come to be second in line to IBM (first in microelectronics). Part of the picture is also that IBM is handling international telecommunication infrastructures in the same sense and magnitude as AT&T and ITT, and is already prepared to operate three new direct tv channels (two for entertainment, one for information) scheduled for 1982, joining production and service under the same control system. Exxon plans to sell 2,000 million dollars worth in microelectronics in 1982, mostly word processors and facsimile equipment.

Not very many know the meaning of the peculiar evolution that is taking place within developed capitalist economies. Media, under the direct influence of transnational imperialists, have misinformed and manipulated world public opinion in the context.

Ideologists and communication experts like de Sola Pool, Bell, Cox, Galbraith, Buckingham, Lerner, Brzozinski and the like, have mixed up the real sense of the process of informatization of society, accelerated under American financial and industrial pressure. They have developed an information ideology based upon a unified pseudo-theory which eliminates any distinction between fundamental science, technical applications and social practice, decontextualizing the political frame of communication and informatics.

Natan Katzman, among others, is opposed to portraying the future as a technological wonderland in which communication techniques could cheaply and painlessly solve major social, economic and educational problems. Communication policies, he warns, are a significant factor in the future shape of social systems.[6]

Karl Schalmann, foreign policy adviser of the Federal Communication Commission and Ithiel de Sola Pool, in charge of the Communication Programme of MIT, hold completely different views. In a report on telecommunications for the 80s they foresee that within five years every developing country will be capable of using the most sophisticated communication systems. Schalmann even pretends that a number of issues raised by the Mac Bride Report and UNESCO debates will become obsolete in the short term, indicating that technological innovations will give the solution to main world problems.[7] They were thinking of a wired world linked through computerized data banks controlled by and from the United States.

The context of the struggle has been pointed out by expert A M Rutkowski of the Federal Communication Commission who, in a paper on *US Policy-Making for the Public International Forum on Communication*, expressed the following:

> *As part of technological revolution in telecommunications, radio and wire transmission, paths are being married to computer systems in such a way that an integrated, global network is developing. Information is becoming the lifeblood of modern society, which must rely on an electronic circulatory systems for its survival. The struggles of the electronic information decades to come will concern effective access to that system and control over the information conveyed.*
>
> *In the 80s this will be the most savage battleground of all, predicts Azziz Mechouar, a Moroccan diplomat who has followed Intergovernmental*

Bureau for Informatics meetings in Rome, an entity which will be the next focal issue of the so-called North-South dialogues.[8]

An alternative to this new subtle way of domination – which includes the erosion of cultures and languages, modes of social behaviour and individual attitudes – is the urgent need of a global struggle in defence of national sovereignty, cultural identity, legitimate traditional values and an autonomous, objective two-way flow of communication, identified by the principles and concepts of the New International Information Order, which rejects the liberal market philosophy stated in the so-called American 'free-flow' doctrine. All these true objectives can be summarized in the quest for national policies of communication, which only a few underdeveloped countries have so far implemented, Cuba amongst them.

We may hold this point as a crucial issue dealing not only with communication and informatics, but also with future world socio-economic options. This is the central question of what is actually happening and has to do with the shape countries and peoples will face during the next 10 years.

Why? Because transnational transactions are wholly dependent on data-based computerized information flows. Economic and financial activities from and into developed industrialized western nations are totally subordinated to microchip and satellite technology. These trends are absolutely necessary to the expansionist strategy of huge monopolist corporations.

The underdeveloped world has not yet been wired to power centre infrastructures in terms of informatics. That is, connected through data banks, guided-wave cables and satellites. Recent actions at international organization level indicate that vested interests are moving in this direction. There is a dire need to interconnect underdeveloped countries to computerized systems the world over. It is quite understandable why this strategy has not yet been implemented, and not for lack of willingness on the part of people unable to know or unaware of what they are up against. Backwardness and dependency are the main reasons.

The so-called Third World represents more than 1,000 million illiterates, 400 million unemployed, 800 million undernourished. As a whole they are affected by a foreign debt that goes beyond 500 billion. These facts do away with the possibility of being interconnected or hooked to automatic networks operated by a small group of western developed countries. In this same sense, transnational power system relations become affected. Thus, the need to maintain *status quo* and neocolonial domination drives these forces to promote apparent interdependence and cooperation, so they can improve infrastructures that cannot be afforded by poor countries. Recent intents to manipulate the second meeting of the IPDC Programme in Acapulco (18–25 January 1982) prove this imperialist strategic approach.

If imperialism and neocolonial relations are to be maintained under actual technological changes, the world needs to be linked to satellites and data banks and to accept the imposition of the free-flow and free-access doctrine. Why is it so important? Nordic countries know, as do Japan and Brazil. They are the first nations to approve a legislation addressed to defend their cultural, economic and political sovereignty.

Canada also knows all too well what this means, because they stated it in the Clyne Report of 1979 when they had been losing annually 30 to 40,000 jobs and $150 to 300 million because of transborder data flow submission to the United States.[9]

What will happen if a number of underdeveloped countries oppose the acceptance of free flow in behalf of legitimate interests and establish autonomous coordinated national communication policies, articulated to educational and cultural sectors within the frame of a general development strategy?

As is known, governments ignore in general the content and magnitude of these flows, considered private investment unavailable out of enterprise control. This is an important question. It could mark the substitution of 'brain drain' by 'knowledge drain' through computerized data banks that do transfer information gathered or developed by experts working within their own countries on behalf of and under the surveillance of transnational corporations. IBM, for example, operates 27 research centres with over 5,000 scientists and high-level technicians in nine Western European countries, whose output nobody measures and which automatically flows to master computers at the matrix enterprise.[10]

Countries that oppose the free-flow doctrine and consider the adoption of convenient national communication policies, are simply breaking transnational corporations' domination system. And this is what the New International Information Order is concerned with. In other words, it stands for the continuation of the decolonization struggle along with the promotion of a New International Economic Order.

Both orders – and struggles – were developed almost 10 years ago by the Non-Aligned Countries Movement. It is important to state that the Movement not only took major steps to build the New Information Order, but has also formally conceptualized, approved and established its basic, fundamental principles, opposed by nature to free flow and all forms of transnational monopolistic and imperialistic domination.

These facts are part of the Movement's history since the Fourth Summit of Heads of State in Algiers (1973). Economic and information orders were consecrated at the Fifth Summit in Colombo (1976) and further stressed at the Sixth Summit in Havana (1979).

These concepts and principles have evolved since the First Meeting of the Intergovernmental Council of the Non-Aligned for Information, held in Tunisia in 1976. The Second Meeting in Havana (April 1978) was a key outcome, taking into account that it agreed to develop the fundamental ideas in which embody the aims, hopes and objectives of the Movement in the field of information and communication. The set of principles were coordinated, arranged and presented for approval to the Foreign Ministers Meeting held in Belgrade (July 1978) and afterwards sanctioned by the Sixth Summit in Havana.

Under political objectives Nos 4 & 5, p 10 of the Cyrus Vance Report on World Communication Problems addressed to the US Congress on 15 January 1979, (the first issued in this field on behalf of a mandate given to the Government by the Foreign Relations Committee of the Senate), the American Secretary of State underlined that the Government should not allow the Non-Aligned Movement to in any way establish alone the principles referred to in a New World Information Order, because it is absolutely necessary to introduce in the Movement's conceptual frame the free-flow doctrine which stands for free market and enterprise.

This apparently irrelevant and innocent semantic issue has inhibited United States private transnational corporations and government from accepting and stimulating multilateral technological transfer and, in this sense, from backing the New Information Order, UNESCO, the MacBride Report and the International Programme for the Development of Communication, otherwise known as IPDC.

Up to now, the United States has not succeeded in co-opting the Non-Aligned Movement's New Order of Information. And it is doubtful they will.

The United States and its allies have openly promised to pay in kind, as US Ambassador to UNESCO and chief delegate to the 21st General Conference at Belgrade, Barbara Newell, untactfully indicated at an internal negotiation meeting with representatives of the Non-Aligned and the Group of 77: 'There is money, but you'll have to drop the so-called principles,' she said to the bewilderment of Third-World ambassadors, among others, Rasghotra from India and Masmoudi from Tunisia.

Up to the present, imperialism has not neutralized the strong commitment of the Non-Aligned Countries towards autonomous equilibrated information, cultural identity and national sovereignty. But they surely have tried hard enough through different ways, like the following:

a) world propaganda campaigns against UNESCO, its Director General and the President of the MacBride Commission.

b) reiterated intents of internal division from within the Non-Aligned Movement.

c) blunt chantages like that organized by the State Department and the World Press Freedom Committee at the so-called Conference of Talloires, one month before the First IPDC Meeting in Paris.

d) continous warnings and threats from high-ranking government officials like Brzezinski, Vance, Sarah Godar Powell, John Reinhardt, Jeanne Kirkpatrick, Elliot Abrams, Bush, Haigh and, finally, President Reagan himself.

e) an official announcement by Abrams at the Sub-commission of External Operations of the Foreign Affairs Committee, in May 1981, warning that the Reagan Administration, the Congress and transnational corporations will jointly and actively oppose the New World Information Order, in defence of the free flow of information.

f) approval by Congress in September 1981 – based on a letter from Reagan to the Speaker of the House of Representatives – of an amendment to the appropriations law giving the Government a mandate, which can only be understood as gross blackmail, to cut off financial contributions to UNESCO and the United Nations if either one of these international bodies should agree on any resolution against or aimed at limiting free flow of information.

g) a spectacular warning by the SmithKline Corporation published in the central pages of *Newsweek* (8 February 1982, pp 85–88) and *Time* magazine (1 February 1982, pp 39–42), entitled 'Danger at the UN'. In this text, Allen Weinstein of the Georgetown University Centre for Strategic and International Studies underlines that with western technical aid we should concentrate on strengthening the media in societies that show some resolve to resist state domination of communications, and deal differently with countries where the government controls the press completely. In this sort of ideological advertising and action guide for the defenders of the so-called economic freedom, Weinstein reiterates that developed countries hold coveted technologies and vital capital as well as their own natural resources and indispensable markets. By selectively offering and withholding our markets, skills and capital, we can convince the often unstable regimes of poor countries that neither stability nor prosperity can be obtained through bureaucratic coercion.Both press and business should recognize the clear convergence of their interests in this field. After mentioning that the Talloires Meeting marks an historic turning point for world press liberties, the document adds that the United States should not feel compelled to continue its generosity toward UN agencies that remain relentlessly hostile to freedom of information and other fundamental principles of democracy. The President of the SmithKline Corporation, Robert F Dee, points out in an adjoining ad that we offer you the ideas referred to as a further investment in a healthier future for America and the world.

Let us mention some particular signs that show the present stand of the New Order of Information and how this relates to the process of global informatization and the imperialist strategy:

1 Allied interest and certain countries within the Group of 77 have been guided by the US State Department to distort the conceptual frame and fundamental principles of the New Order by way of trying to introduce the free-flow doctrine in joint documents along with the Non-Aligned Movement at United Nations and UNESCO meetings. This was the case during the First Council Meeting of the IPDC (Paris, 17 June 1981), pressed through a round table convened in a provocative manner by *International Herald Tribune*.

2 A resolution approved at the 21st General Conference of UNESCO at Belgrade to elaborate a Declaration on the New Order was intended as an opportunity to distort the New Order's principles by introducing in it the 'free-flow' and 'free-access' doctrine.

3 The New Orders principles were strongly attacked by the American media during the first meeting of the IPDC, without being able to obscure its role and presence within the main texts and final report. The same thing happened at the second IPDC meeting at Acapulco.

4 New pragmatic tendencies appearing within UNESCO's communication sector favoured a Colloquium on Information Interchange in Paris (27–30

October 1981), which helped to get together high transnational corporation representatives, international financing institutions and some Third-World countries interested in operative technological transfer. Results were intended for the second meeting of IPDC. Amongst them were the promotion of bilateral cooperation through private interests, the acceptance of the free-flow doctrine, the announcement that big corporations were prepared to contribute to the developing of telecommunications infrastructures in Third-World countries and the launching of a project, supported by Sri Lanka, to interconnect in the short term underdeveloped systems to the Intelsat satellite. An urgent and fruitful mission, with members from the Colloquium, was sent to Washington to explore its disposition. Its report at the IPDC Meeting in Acapulco was energetically questioned and opposed by Cuba, with the backing of India and France. It was agreed to carry on the so-called study, but with a controversial question mark on it.

5 In December 81 a monitoring group assisted by 14 outstanding regional communication experts met in Quito, Ecuador to follow up the resolutions and recommendations of the Intergovernmental Conference on National Policies of Communication in Latin America and the Caribbean. A representative of UNESCO's secretariat stated firmly that international institutions are now giving operative steps to promote practical solutions to solve financial difficulties and that actual trends lead to a close interconnection between private and public sectors. This approach was understood as demanding pressures in behalf of a 'Marshall Plan of Telecommunications', the imposition of a 'wired world' linked to Intelsat, and the distortion of the principles of the New International Information Order under the influence of 'free flow'.

In the final report the experts agreed to oppose these positions, and questioned UNESCO on the understanding that those who in the region fight for implementing a New International Information Order are in line not with an international organization but with a strategical project, and that this fundamental aim was going to be carried out with or without UNESCO if the institution gives away its militant defence of such historical cause and limits itself to a conformist, technocratic and depoliticized attitude.[11]

6 Finally, the IPDC Meeting at Acapulco showed the strong efforts made by American imperialist transnationals to curve the New Order's principles through the open offering of financial help, which introduced a market mood during the debates, rejected by a number of countries.

The trading of telecommunication equipment and assistance from monopolistic sources was defeated once more, though aggressive pressures were put on African and Asian countries. Hopefully, even though there was an initial internal division amongst Latin Americans, Africans and the Group of 77 – as there also was within western countries – unity stood in behalf of principles, cultural identity and national sovereignty, backed by the Non-Aligned Movement and the socialist group.

The so-called Third-World countries, which are beginning to awake to the meaning of the deal offered by imperialism, relied once more on the defence of national policies of communication, endogenous effort, self-determination and horizontal solidarity, expressed in, by and through the New Order's concepts and principles. They knew the price to be paid back was too high and its effects irreversible. A number of countries now know better about these contingencies. They know, for instance, what Isaac Asimov concluded when he put his finger on the problem in an article entitled *Disassembling the Assembly Line:*

> *The development of microcomputers has made it possible to equip machines with enough of a brain to make them capable of fulfilling assembly line requirements. Nowadays robots can work longer and better than human beings. Being out of work and on government handouts is not a pleasant result. So when technological change comes, other things must change with it. There must be matching social change.[12]*

Monopolistic capitalism is not prepared for that kind of change, nor does it consider it desirable. They knew all the time that a growing labour rationalization of the economy through informatization of society would become structural and permanent. And that it would deepen antagonistic unsolvable contradictions and accelerate social, political and class struggle to a point not considered before.

To keep the unemployed safely under control, at home and abroad in more than 130 countries, is why Reagan's Administration has adopted fascism and military repression as a way of government. In a recent book, Herbert Schiller states that computerized communications are of inestimable value for transnational consortiums and their basic structures, banking, advertising, market research enterprises, travel agencies and internationally deployed armed forces.[13]

For the weak, Schiller stresses, the perspective is a closer integration to an unequal relatiohs system. Dependency, instead of lessening, tends to expand further. New technologies allow transnationals to reinforce their international operations and keep control over the world domination system and international division of labour.

In these and other texts, Schiller has mentioned the absolute need to adopt autonomous national communication policies and to initiate international systematic efforts to develop models, codes and convenient conditions before informatization processes are introduced in the Third-World countries. We are threatened, he says, with the substitution of a New International Information Order by a New International Electronic Order with a totally different nature and aims.

We come again to the heart of the question: the political reorganization underlying production-relations change in the capitalist system, and the worrysome steps already taken by transnational monopolistic powers to solve their unsurmountable antagonistic contradictions.

What kind of response, not taking into account political propaganda or psychological warfare, can be given by imperialism to this threatening situation that places in peril domination and corporate systems alike at the very height of its scientific and technological strength? The answer is disinformation and violence. On the one hand, to hide real issues from public world opinion, to mystify and disguise effects and aims of industrial and social changes. On the other hand, to threaten with retaliaton, to provoke an histerical anticommunist mood so as to paralyze any counteraction from the Third-World countries, and even threaten Western European countries with economic pressures.

This wide spectrum of effects and consequences microelectronics has upon labour has been clearly demonstrated by Juan Rada, of ILO, whose valuable research in this field decisively contributes to demystify such a complex subject and helps to put the problem in the right context to be fully understood.

Knowledge industry, computer age, technotronic society, global village, are some of the terms used by the ideological promoters of this silent shift which is altering the international division of labour and turning habits, attitudes and values upside down.

The key point is that scientific-technical development in the electronics field goes beyond the bounds of technology to become the centre of great debates on the future of man, the survival of cultural pluralism and the balance in international relations.

The subject is no longer limited to sophisticated innovations. This unsuspected dimension acquires crucial importance when the knowledge accumulated in transnational enterprises' data banks and the computerized transmission of messages and information of every type begins to be viewed as essential to national economic progress and autonomy.

96

Science and technology are tools which can promote or hold back human development, depending on the systems, objectives and contexts in which they are applied. Basic economic and social structures decide the trends. They can promote liberation or increase inequality and dependency.

It cannot be forgotten – nor can one overlook the fact – that producers of guided missiles, military satellites and sophisticated modern weapons, are the same consortiums which control the international information system and manufacture the electronic components on which instantaneous global transmission is based. Nor can one fail to note that these gigantic enterprises are controlled by a small number of financial groups through a complicated system of investment diversification and horizontal-vertical relations.

Even for most of the experts and observers in this field, confrontation between American imperialism and the New International Information Order was until recently not a very well known issue, and still is a hidden one, at large, for the international community. Some specialists think it is just a political question in no way referring to technological impact and socio-economic change.

We think it does. First of all, there's too much involved. It should be crucial to ascertain before hand, for instance, whether a certain global strategy is to be safely implemented by huge transnational corporations.

Summarizing the problem, if an unrestricted acceptance of free transborder data flow is not guaranteed, information-linked projects will need to proceed on an irregular bilateral basis; time will be lost by capitalist oligarchies and the prospect of a 'wired world'.

One reason for believing that Third-World countries are becoming more sensitive about informatics is the steady development of endogenous experience and 'know-how' in some Asian and Latin-American countries, such as India, Brazil and Cuba. This is not only concerned with equipment design and production, but with the development of proper and autonomous 'software' or logistics, without which a real independent operation cannot be fulfilled.

Already different degrees of advancement can be measured in this particular field, not very well known in general by the rest of the underdeveloped countries. This is a very important outcome because it could possibly be considered as a favourable step towards horizontal cooperation and an example that cadre formation and independent manufacturing is not at all forbidden to those outside the western developed area.

Another possibility that should be increasingly considered is the emerging situation created by contradictions between the United States and the OECD nations, the willingness of European countries to foster their capabilities in informatics from independent positions, and the need to assess not only industrial challenge in microelectronics, but cultural values and national identity as well. These tendencies are quite clear, most of all in France, the United Kingdom and Italy.

It should also be stated that the new positions being assumed by the so-called Third-World countries express themselves in the sustained willingness to celebrate in 1984 the Second SPIN Conference in Havana, already agreed upon and reaffirmed by Latin-American countries at a regional meeting in Santiago de Chile in November 1981. Some five other regional meetings will take place under the auspices of the Intergovernmental Bureau for Informatics (IBI), the next one to be in Africa. It should be mentioned, that the initial announcement of the Second SPIN was made by the President of Mexico, López Portillo, in 1981 at a meeting attended by nearly 30 world personalities.

The Second World Conference on Informatics Policies and Strategies will be devoted to development in the Third World. In this particular frame, underdeveloped countries will come to deal not only with real technological transfer, but also with its applied frames of action, including socio-economic consequences and the analysis of North-South and South-South possibilities of concrete understanding.

Cuba, in this context, could be in a position to share its own experience as regards how, being still after 23 years of aggression a blockaded and hostile nation, it managed to build an industrial endogenous infrastructure in informatics, and developed the National Institute for Automated and Computerized Systems (INSAC) to guide state policy in this field.

It is also convenient to mention that our country nearly reinvented minicomputers because it did not have any other choice. So, that's why we design hardware and software and build, with 85% of the components from our own sources, the equipment and complementary technology we use and export. The latest series, the CID/300–10, has been admitted as a prototype by the COMECON or mutual assistance socialist economic group.

The meaning of informatization and the sense the struggle against 'free flow' is taking on, is at the heart of the issue. This subject was dealt with by us in a couple of analytical works, one entitled *Informatization of Society, New Way of Dependency,* published by the Latin-American Institute of Transnational Studies (ILET), Mexico, 1979, the other, a paper concerned with the transnational information system, written for the Conference on Communication in the 80s, convened by the Annenberg School of Communications in Philadelphia.

It is no longer possible to hide the true questions referring to informatics and socio-political change. There have been omissions, disinformation and diversionism during the past 25 years, with the help of certain well known specialists working for the industrial-military complex. In some cases, outstanding analysts like Alvin Toffler even admit that few know what's happening. As he dramatically points out:

Hidden inside our advance to a new production system is a potential for social change so breathtaking in scope that few among us have been willing to face its meaning.

Toffler adds that as tiny microprocessors turn up in more products, they replace an impressive number of components and moving parts. Vast changes in the technosphere and the infosphere converge to change the way we make goods; in brief, we are revolutionizing the deep structure of production, sending currents of change through every layer of society.

Toffler, author of *Future Shock,* gives a very clear picture in *The Third Wave* concerning the effects of microelectronic innovations:

What is certain is that both the office and the factory are destined to be revolutionized in the decades ahead. . . .this adds up to nothing less than a wholly new mode of production for society . . .this step carries with it indescribably complex implications. It will affect not only such things as the level of employment and the structure of industry but also the distribution of political and economic power, the size of our work units, the international division of labour, the role of women in the economy, the nature of work and the divorce of producer from consumer.[14]

Perhaps Toffler has not received much serious attention either because he is not an academician and his works are published as pocket books sensationally advertised and commonly distributed at airports and supermarkets, or because he has not gone to the ultimate roots of the problem, and disguises the very causes of historical processes.

We are now beginning to comprehend why and how these changing forces are interconnected with big corporations' long-range strategies and their global reach, so well-dissected by experts like Barnett and Muller, and more recently by Cees Hamelink, who has devoted serious research to determining interactions between high finance and microelectronics.

Though we are coming closer to the subject, still there are not enough experts or official advisers who could deal at the same time with technology and politics. And this is most needed to sense that the real magnitude of the issue is not only manpower or labour levels being affected, not even the bold hegemony of a sole country, but the drastic changes that are taking place within the capitalist system itself.

To call attention to this unawareness it could be mentioned that more than 600 delegates attended the Second Meeting of the Economists of the Third World at Havana in May 1981. And not even a single paper dealt with the effects of technological innovations, though the event had had a very high academic and professional level, proving that this particular area urgently needs attention if we are to decide where we are heading and what we shall do about it.

Coming back to the point, the mere existence of the market system economy lies at the bottom of the problem. What actual changes really reveal is the real threat of cultural homogenization, totalizing power controls, radical restructuring of the service sector, the acute shrinking of the manufacturing sector, and a completely new economic phenomenon like simultaneous inflation and stagnation. Not only continuous proliferation of automated, robotized production units operated by a few high-level specialists can be identified as dangerous trends, but other worrying contradictions also begin to appear.

Andrew Robertson of the Polytechnic of Central London reminds us in a work on *Technological Innovations and their Social Impacts* that in 1962 the Kennedy Administration was warned of mass unemployment arising from the advent of the 'automatic factory', and that 30% of the 6.6 million unemployed in the US at that date were victims of automation.[15]

President Kennedy, says Robertson, set up a special advisory committee to deal with the problem. Today the figures are 10 million and still growing, because there is a marked privatization of the public sector, a steady super-concentration in financial and microelectronics areas, and a strong impulse of these trends under Reagan, who said when he took over: 'The problems are not within the Government; the problem is the Government. Private enterprise will solve it.' And, as is known, business only cares about customers and profit, not about people.

Problems in the information and communication fields are no longer limited to underdeveloped context. Cultural aggression and changing patterns of life and behaviour will not only exclusively affect the 'have-nots'. Applied microinformatics and hence capitalist market strategy involve every other country. The true possibility of a coming 'wired world', controlled by huge transnational monopolistic enterprises, endangers everyone in the sense that we are all in some way interdependent whether we like it or not.

Today's realities indicate that actual efforts are being made to modernize market economy systems. This is to upgrade production, management and control mechanisms. Within this frame it is quite clear that informatics is being used with the purpose of preserving and enhancing *status quo*, while inducing new types of production relations aimed against labour as an organized force based on class differences. Its impact at working level can be measured in terms of drastic rationalization, erosion of working abilities, disappearance of basic functions and structural unemployment.

It can be safely stated that there exists a vast campaign of disinformation and diversionism through every media available to demobilize class consciousness. Why? Because the same elements used to improve communications are being applied by power centres to introduce negative desocializing effects upon working relations and to disrupt union organization.

The new technological processes can be applied to any logical sequence. At every level in any type of function, they deal with information. The same mechanism used in data or news transfer can control automated industries. Basically, they serve an equal role in modern printing as they do in decision-taking at business and administrative or bureaucratic level.

It is important to appreciate that there is an ever widening gap between the socializing consequences of the production forces and production relations – what Toffler naively terms 'divorce between producer and consumer'. Interimperialist market struggle has pushed forward technological innovations. But it has gone too far to accommodate social change and establish coherent policies, to assimilate a turnover that goes out of hand and gives way to unpredictable developments.

It is a fact that industrialized capatilist countries have not been able to promote adequate new social values or assess the transition to a computerized society without heavy socio-political costs. The outcome will undoubtedly be deepening differences, social unrest and, eventually, a more pronounced political consciousness and the reinforcement of class struggle.

Katzman, project director for the Corporation for Public Broadcasting, thinks that new communication technologies do not automatically solve – and may aggravate – social problems because of unequal use. According to research done for Stanford University, new communication technologies and techniques create new information gaps before old ones close.

The widening gap, he says, tends to be associated more with initial economic status than with personal ability. He further stresses that when communication techniques are applied to social problems, the political implications of the widening gap between information-rich and -poor becomes critical.[16]

Elie Abel, Chandler Professor of Communications, points out the same negative tendencies in a paper presented at the University of Virginia under the title *Looking Ahead From the 20th Century*.[17] We are confronted with social and political decisions by the transformations imposed upon us by the new information technologies, says Patrick Roger of the University of Grenoble in a research on socio-cultural development alternatives in a changing world, a project under the auspices of the United Nations University.[18]

Imperialist powers are beginning to dawn on these realities and now aim to neutralize upsurging forces. That is why they promote operational, obsolete technology transfer addressed to the so-called Third World. The plan is to establish a well-rooted telecommunications infrastructure before national communication policies can be opposed to unrestricted transnational operations.

Monopolistic corporations earn from 50 to 80% of their incomes from investments and business abroad. Operational systems, commercialization, stock and exchange, management, banking and economic controls are actually based on informatics and satellite communication, as universal credit cards, advertising and legal advice, prime export activity of the New York industrial community.[19] At the same expansion rate, advertising agencies follow transnational corporations wherever they go.[20] They collect, mainly from North-American sources, 65% of total commercial publicity, which went up to more than $100,000 million in 1980[21], and keeps growing at an annual rate of 15%.

Today's world is represented by 158 countries which do care about their integrity, traditions and sovereignty. Therefore, interdependence is a must for the functioning of operative transnational communications networks if world management and corporate benefits are to be maintained.

But there is quite a problem because underdeveloped countries have only access to a mere 10% of total media and communications facilities. This part of humanity want their share to guarantee their development and protect their identity. These perspectives create additional tensions, besides those emerging from the new world equilibrium of forces, the advancement of socialism in different regions and the persistent actions of national liberation movements in Asia, Africa and Latin America.

Decolonization, therefore, needs to be extended to cover other fields than mere information or news to cope with every kind of data transfer. We are summoned to move from the microcosm of messages to the macrocosm of social and political action because informatics is engulfing everything. The fight for decolonization in the information field is closely connected with that of peace, development and the right to work and live without being telemanipulated by an elite of monopolistic power centres listed by *Fortune* magazine. This is our first task if we are going to have a real two-way flow communication, which can only be strengthened through endogenous effort and autonomous policy-making under international solidarity and mutual unconditioned cooperation.

There are some specific ways by which a real contribution could be made to foster decolonization in the information and communication fields, a process that will affect future trends of life on a global scale:

a) to defend and promote the New International Information Order, based upon principles established by the Non-Aligned Movement, and opposed to imperialism, monopolism and neocolonialism.

b) to assume as a basic reference the Non-Aligned Resolution on the New International Information Order approved at the Fourth Intergovernmental Meeting in Baghdad, which gathers the fundamental concepts approved by a hundred countries. This point will have significant importance in debates at the next (22nd) General Conference of UNESCO, where North-American chantage will be put on trial.

c) to strengthen the International Programme for the Development of Communication (IPDC). This project came out as a cooperation programme by and for underdeveloped countries with the contributions of progressive and socialist countries. One of its aims is to stimulate the adoption of national policies of communication articulated to cultural and educational sectors, in line with adequate infrastructures within the frame of a general development strategy.

d) to study thoroughly the negative economic and political implications of the 'free-flow' and 'free-access' doctrine, and its possible consequences for communication, education and culture.

e) to follow up changes being introduced in capitalist production relations systems after the massive dissemination of microelectronics and computer-chips techniques, which allows financial super-concentration, operative decentralization, vertical and horizontal multisectorial investment and the unification of production and service sectors, affecting union stability, manpower levels and the international division of labour.

f) to study the socio-economic impact of microelectronic innovations, taking into account that sophisticated technology as computers, microprocessors, coaxial and guided-wave cables and remote-sensing satellites do not only radically transform known ways of transmission of data, news and messages, but alter the character, functions and purpose of information flows and contents. These processes could introduce extremely dangerous new forms of neocolonial dependency and cultural domination.

References

1 Bruno Lussato, *Le défi informatique,* Librairie Arthème Fayard, Paris, 1981, p 11.

2 *Toward an American Agenda for a New World Order of Communications,* US National Commission for UNESCO, Conference Report, January 1980, pp 12–13.

3 Kaarle Nordenstreng, *Actual Problems Concerning NIIO,* February 1982, p 64, mimeo.

4 Eli Ginzberg and George Vojta, *The Service Sector in the US Economy,* American Scientific, New York, March 1981, pp 33–38.

5 Dennis Redmont, 'North-South Talks Enter Computer Age' in *International Herald Tribune,* 23 June 1981, p 9.

6 Natan Katzman, 'The Impact of Communication Technology: Promises and Prospects' in *Journal of Communication,* Autumn 1974, pp 47–58.

7 E L Nickremasinghe, *Elements Related to Information Issues to be Considered by Non-Aligned and Group of 77 Representatives,* working paper presented by Sri Lanka at the plenary meeting of the Group of 77, UNESCO, Paris, 24 June 1980, p 4.

8 Dennis Redmont, *op.cit.*

9 Anthony Smith, *The Geopolitics of Information,* London, 1981.

10 *Newsweek,* European edition, 15 October 1980.

11 *Informe Final de la Primera Reunión del Grupo de Monitoria sobre el Seguimiento de la Conferencia Internacional sobre Políticas de Comunicación en América Latina y el Caribe de la UNESCO,* Oficina Regional de Comunicación Social de la UNESCO para América Latina y el Caribe, Quito, Ecuador, 30 Noviembre–2 Diciembre 1981, pp 29–30.

12 Isaac Asimov, 'Disassembling the Assembly Line' in *American Way* magazine, American Airlines, Vol 14 No 5, May 1981.

13 Herbert I Schiller, *Who Knows: Information in the Age of the Fortune 500,* Alex Publications, New York, 1981.

14 Alvin Toffler, *The Third Wave,* Bantam Books, New York, April 1981, pp 193–220.

15 Andrew Robertson, 'Technological Innovations and Their Social Impacts' in *International Social Science Journal,* Vol 33 No 3, 1981, p 431.

16 Natan Katzman, *op.cit.*

17 Elie Abel, *Looking Ahead From the 20th Century,* Conference on Communications in the 21st Century, Richmond, Virginia, 1–2 April 1981, pp 10–17.

18 Roger Patrick, *Le défi informational dans un monde en metamorphose,* the United Nations University, Tokyo, HSDRSCA–67F/UNUP–297, 1981, pp 1–4.

19 Eli Ginzberg and George Vojta, *op.cit.,* p 38.

20 Herbert I Schiller, *La communication suit le capital,* MacBride Commission Reports no 47, 1979, pp 1–13.

21 *Nouvel Observateur,* 'Hors d'ouvre 1979', Paris p 44.

Communication Satellites:
a Third-World Perspective

Neville D Jayaweera
Associate General Secretary,
World Association for Christian Communication

Introduction

Science and technology can be borrowed, imported and adapted from abroad. But ultimately creativity from within is the only answer. For development, essentially, is not a matter of technology or GNP, but the growth of a new consciousness, the movement of the human mind, the uplifting of the human spirit, the infusion of human confidence.

Everett Kleinjans[1] (President, East-West Centre, Honolulu, 1975.)

We may accept this quotation as a useful jumping-off ground for our discussion, not because we can all share Kleinjan's understanding of what development is 'essentially' about, but because his rejection of science, technology and GNP as constituting the essential determinants of development, is by itself significant. Firstly, because it is a formal admission of the failure of a particular development-cum-communication ideology, i.e., the 'modernization' paradigm, that emanated from the United States in the 50s and the 60s and holds sway in many developing countries to this day.[2] Secondly, because it comes from the head of an institution which, since its inception by an Act of Congress in 1960, has been veritably the bastion of that ideology, at least in its communication aspect.

Let me dwell a moment on the circumstances that led Kleinjans to make this pronouncement.

In 1964 a conference was held in the East-West Centre in Honolulu which was intended to develop a global consensus on the role of communication in development. To this end were brought together the purveyors of 'development' and 'communication' wisdom conventional at that time – Max Millikan and Harry Oshima, *et al.*, on development theory, and Daniel Lerner and Wilbur Schramm, *et al.*, on communication theory. The consensus achieved at this consultation was published in 1965 with a foreword from President

106

Lyndon Johnson.[3] Reduced to its most simplistic expression, the consensus developed at this conference reads something like this. Developing countries remain underdeveloped because of their 'traditional' ways. If they are to 'develop', that is, to become like western industrial societies, their 'traditional' habits of thinking and behaving have to be changed drastically. This can be achieved most quickly through mass communication. Therefore, if 'development' or 'modernization' is to be achieved, heavy investments have to be undertaken on the development of mass communication systems, principally radio. If only developing countries could be persuaded to invest in efficient delivery systems, then, notwithstanding the content of the message, the very presence of the mass medium would be adequate to set in motion those socio-economic processes that would ultimately 'modernize' their societies.

During the decade that followed, both the 'modernization' and 'development communication' concepts received wide acceptance within the Third World. Massive investments in mass media infrastructure were willingly undertaken. Transmitters, transistor radios and tv sets were multiplied many times over. For instance, between 1963 and 1973 the number of radio receivers increased by 300% in Africa, by 450% in Asia and by 250% in Latin America.[4] However, out of this injection of 'communication' into the system, 'development and modernization' did not result in proportion to expectations. For instance, if we take two key indicators of economic growth, *viz.*, increases in per capita food production and increases in the share of world trade over the same period, it will be found that the developing countries recorded negative or negligible growth rates and that communication correlated to development in an inverse ratio.[5] Granted that not even the most die-hard modernization addict would claim precise correlations between mass media variables and development, although Daniel Lerner tried to do precisely that, the general picture that emerged after a decade was that mass media delivery systems did not necessarily beget the kind of development that was sought. What *did* emerge was the realization that 'development' was a more complex phenomenon than could be compassed within a few simple variables like foreign aid, capital investments, management, communication, productivity, etc., and that it required a far wider and deeper strategy of social and political engineering than had been imagined earlier. It was the failure of the development paradigm of the 60s, i.e., the 'growth' and 'trickle down' model, that led the UN, on the completion of the First Development Decade, to launch the Second Development Decade, with a heavy emphasis on 'distribution' and 'equity' as distinct from 'growth'.

The initiative taken by the East-West Centre and Wilbur Schramm, *et al.*, in 1975 to summon another conference in Honolulu, of almost the same theoreticians who met there in 1964 to map out a strategy for communication and development, was largely a response to the same set of facts that prompted the UN to launch the Second Development Decade, *viz.*, the failure of the development paradigm of the 60s. The modernization theorists were meeting to ask 'what went wrong'. And this is the confession they made: 'The past decade did not produce the enhanced quality of life that we had hoped for 10 years ago. Even the impressive gains of GNP in many Third-World countries evaporated when restated in per capita terms, for these economic gains were largely swallowed up by greater increases in population. In several poor countries around the world, the quality of life today is, if anything, down.'[6] The pronouncement from Kleinjans in his opening address to the group, quoted at the beginning of this paper, had already set the parameters for the discussion that followed.

Relevance of satellites to the development–communication debate

I have taken some time going over the development paradigm formalized at the East-West Centre in 1964 and abandoned by its very proponents a decade later, because it seems to me that another decade later, on the threshold of 1984, we are witnessing a reversal to the same development-communication paradigm. Except that the tools and the prophets of the 80s are different. In the 60s the tools were radio and tv. In the 80s they will be satellites. In the 60s the prophets came from the behavioural sciences – economics, sociology, etc. In the 80s the prophets are technologists and engineers. But basically the argument is the same: 'Development is something that can be stimulated and engendered through mass communication. The more penetrating, the more widespread, the more efficient the delivery system, the more easily the ultimate development goals can be realized.' One senses the same retreat from complexity that characterized development-communication thinking in the 60s.

At this point it will be useful if we state objectively what specific Third-World needs the advocates of communication satellites believe the new technology will be able to satisfy. The following come to mind as being the principal needs that satellites, by virtue of their special characteristics, are said to be able to meet more cost-effectively than existing terrestrial systems.[7]

1 National integration

Many Third-World countries, either by reason of their immensity and geographical dispersal like India and Indonesia, or by reason of their heterogeneous social composition or because of natural barriers like vast expanses of forests, deserts or mountains, are yet to be integrated into a single polity. The construction of roads and railways, the laying of telephone lines, and the construction of transmitting stations will take a long time and consume meagre capital resources. Meanwhile, domestic distribution satellites can perform this function much more cost-effectively.

2 Administrative effectiveness

As a corollary to 1 above, administrative integration and effectiveness is hampered. The bureaucracy tends towards concentration and higher effectiveness in the metropolis, and declines outwards.

3 Delivery of education, both formal and non-formal including teacher training

The shortage of schools, teachers, equipment and buildings is chronic in most Third-World countries. Satellites have the capacity to multiply these meagre resources at a fraction of their terrestrial costs.

4 Delivery of agricultural extension

As in the area of education, effective agricultural extension work is hampered by the lack of trained extension workers, the lack of transport, the inability to have as many demonstration plots as are needed, etc. All this can be overcome through satellites.

5 Delivery of family-planning programmes

It is claimed by many development economists that the greatest single impediment to development in the Third World is population growth which every year either outstrips or at least equals economic growth. Family planning is therefore seen by them to constitute the centrepiece of any long-term economic strategy. But the crucial question underlying all family-planning programmes is the one concerning communication. It is claimed that satellites are the answer.

6 Delivery of medical- and health-care services

What has been said of educational, agricultural and family-planning extension is equally true of medical and health care. The same infrastructural and personnel inadequacies baulk the delivery of adequate diagnostic and curative services from the metropolis, where a certain volume of professional skills is concentrated, to the outlying provinces where they are grossly inadequate or totally absent. Such skills as are available can be multiplied and dispersed through a domestic distribution satellite. Additionally, by linking to a global satellite network like the Intelsat system, the limited professional staff concentrated in a Third-World capital city can have instantaneous access to the most sophisticated and skilled consultative services available in any major global medical centre, obviating the need to transfer patients over vast distances and enabling a constant upgrading of skills at the periphery.

7 Isolation from marketing information, both national and international

A modern economy must have access to and supply the most up-to-date data instantaneously and on call, both to suppliers and customers abroad and at home. The speed of modern international commerce has rendered telegraph and all narrow-band telephonic communication, including telex, using short-wave frequencies, almost as obsolete as surface mail. Unless entrepreneurs, banks and firms have access to data banks and facsimile services through computers linked to satellites using digital transmissions, the international market would collapse. On a much smaller scale, this would be equally true of the domestic market.

8 Region-specific cultural programming

One of the major shortcomings of nearly all Third-World radio and tv networks is that they are mostly centrally controlled and put out blanket programmes often ignoring cultural diversity within the national community. The solution to this consists of providing as many regional radio and tv channels as there are cultural groupings. Quite clearly, this would be impossible through terrestrial systems, because of the costs involved. But, with the arrival of direct broadcast and multi-beam high-gain satellites, each cultural and linguistic group can be serviced through just one satellite, without the aid even of a ground station or a terrestrial network.

9 Political and a social pluralism

Of the approximately 110 Third-World countries recognized by the UN as being Less Developed Countries, all, except perhaps six among them, have autocratic governments (either of the left or of the right), controlled economies (either capitalist or socialist) and closed societies. It is claimed that communication satellites will seriously erode the power and durability of such systems. Once a national telephone network is linked to an international direct-dialling network through a satellite, the barriers to communication are breached forever and the official censor stands in risk of his job. Similarly, through access to outside programme material beamed down from direct broadcast satellites, any closed society must begin to breathe again.

10 Participation as a development tool

Most Third-World societies are highly hierarchical. Planning and decision-making are centralized and remote from the people. There are neither political nor societal mechanisms that enable the widest possible community to participate in either the political or the production process. This is one of the reasons to which low productivity in these societies is attributed. Normally, securing participation in broad societal processes is a highly complicated enterprise in social engineering. But technologists see in communication satellites the final answer. What is unique in the new generation of satellites is that they enable interactive communication. As far back as ATS 1, which was launched in 1966 and later became Peacesat, interactive communication on an audio frequency was possible. But now interactive video communication is possible and within the next decade the wristwatch interactive receiving-transmitting terminal could be a reality.[8] So the utopia of participation which has challenged and perplexed ideologists, social scientists and politicians from the time of the panchayats of the Aryans and the Greek city states, down through the early Christian Church and the Presbyterians to the communes of Mao Tse Tung, is now said to be instantly realizable through the mediation of the communication satellite.

11 The capacity to cope with natural disasters

Many Third-World countries are notoriously prone to natural disasters such as cyclones, typhoons, tornadoes and tidal waves, floods and droughts, and earthquakes and famines. When disaster strikes, the capacity to organize relief on an adequate scale depends on the efficiency of the local telephone and transport systems. The availability of the communication satellite alters all that. Not only can relief be summoned speedily but the extent and severity of the disaster can be communicated in all its starkness to the whole world, thereby enabling the mobilization of maximum support. Additionally and more importantly, the onset of some of these disasters, such as a typhoon, a tidal wave or even a famine, can be sensed out by satellites and predicted well ahead of the event so that there is maximum preparedness when the disaster actually strikes.

I have stated the case for communication satellites in the Third World at its strongest and in the categories in which it is generally seen by technologists, in order that we may mount a comprehensive critique thereof later on in this paper. But before we do so, it will help to remind ourselves that, currently, establishment and technological thinking is heavily in favour of using communication satellites in a development-support role in the Third World. This articulation comes mostly from technologists. Perhaps few have been so enthusiastic in their claims on behalf of communication satellites in the Third World as Arthur Clarke, the man who in 1945 first provided the theoretical basis for a satellite in geostationary orbit. Here is an example of his claims. 'To many developing countries satellites are *essential*. . . indeed for such countries satellites could be a matter of life and death. To put it as dramatically as possible, unless major investments are made in space, millions are going to die, or eek out brief and miserable lives. And most of those millions will be in the Third World.'[9] Besides Arthur Clarke, there are others from the Third World, who are protagonists for communication satellites. Two outstanding names, both Indians, are the late Dr Vikram Sarabhai of the Indian Space Research Organization and Dr Yash Pal, one-time Head of the Space Applications Centre at Ahmedabad and Secretary General of the 1982 UN Space Conference. Vikram Sarabhai was convinced that communication satellites would enable Third-World countries to leapfrog over decades of obsolescent technology with which the developed countries are now burdened.[10] Yash Pal even goes to the extent of ridiculing those who see in communication satellites a vehicle for cultural imperialism.[11] Perhaps somewhat surprisingly, but significantly, the prophet of radio and mass communication in the 60s, Wilbur Schramm, argues the case for communication satellites with a greater caution than he showed when he pleaded the cause of radio two decades earlier. He says: 'The almost miraculous development of the communication satellite, and its spectacular capacity for delivering information over vast areas have overleaped anything any planner, two decades ago, felt he needed to be concerned with. We are living and shall continue to live for some years in the shadow of those three remarkable years, 1945, 1946 and 1947, the years of the satellite, the transistor and the computer. . . This is to the credit of our technology. But we have by no means thought through the related questions of how and whether. . . we must ask these questions both about the satellite and what it carries, how, when and whether to use satellites, and how, when and whether to use television in connection with it, for the purposes we have in mind.'[12]

Empirical evidence concerning communication satellite usage in the Third World

As I have mentioned in the foregoing section, the susceptibility to satellite usage for development is fairly widespread in the Third World. We may note very briefly, the following instances of usage either already completed, still in operation or planned for the immediate future.

The first communication satellites to be used for experiments in a development-support role were ATS 1 and ATS 3. They were launched by the US in 1966 and 1967 respectively and were used for interactive voice communication by the University of South Pacific, in Alaska for health-care delivery to remote areas and by Peacesat for international conferencing.[13] Then came ATS 6, a more powerful satellite, capable of carrying video channels and a larger volume of communication traffic, but not interactive. This satellite was used in India in 1975–76 for the SITE experiment, which to this day has been the single largest attempt to deliver development programming via a satellite.[14] The first Third-World country to own a satellite for domestic communication purposes was Indonesia – Palapa 1 inaugurated in 1976. Palapa is tied to a terrestrial microwave system covering the whole republic.[15] The first Arab satellite was expected to be launched by the end of 1982, mainly for intra-regional telephony. It is claimed that Arabsat will contribute to the development of the educational and social welfare of the Arab states.[16] The University of the West Indies, after experimenting with ATS 3 and ATS 6 in 1978 is now seeking the collaboration of AID for investigating the feasibility of having a satellite system for educational purposes in the Caribbean.[17] A similar project is being planned for the Philippines.[18] In addition there are several Third-World countries, such as Algeria, Nigeria, Brazil and Peru, who are already making use of transponder facilities leased from the Intelsat system for their domestic communication and development needs.[19] Domestic satellite systems are also planned for Chile, Nigeria and Zaire.[20]

This is merely an inventory of the better known instances of Third-World satellite usage. Unfortunately, except in the case of the SITE experiment in India, none of these instances has been competently researched by persons devoid of vested interests in their perpetuation. At least, if they have been researched, their findings have not been circulated too widely. The literature widely available concerning them has been put out mostly by suppliers of equipment and commercial interests.

However, SITE is a notable exception. This was an experiment for using a communication satellite for delivering and generating development over the vast rural sector of the sub-continent of India. It had been planned almost 10 years before it was carried out, by an interdisciplinary group of technologists, broadcasters, development economists, anthropologists, agronomists and administrators. The experiment was accompanied by an intensive and highly sophisticated monitoring exercise undertaken by a research unit lodged in the project itself. This built-in evaluation unit has placed before us a vast volume of research findings.[21] However, it is almost impossible to express within the scope of a limited article like this anything more than a distillation of this mass of data. Let me try to sketch out the broad outlines of the picture that emerged.

The objectives of SITE, reduced to their most basic terms were:[22]
1 the improvement of primary school education;
2 facilitating teacher training;
3 the diffusion of improved agricultural practices;
4 the extension of health, hygiene and nutrition;
5 the extension of family planning;
6 national integration.

These objectives were to be promoted during the period of 1 August 1975 to 31 July 1976 in 2,330 villages scattered over 20 districts and six states of India, by linking thousands of community tv sets to the ATS 6 communication satellite.

On the completion of the experiment, the evaluators found:[23]

1 In respect of primary school education – that children and teachers responded to tv attentively, that very little gains were registered in science, social studies and mother tongue, that children did not learn from the content of science education programmes, but that the 'general understanding and information-seeking behaviour of the children had changed.'[24] Also, very importantly, that 'there were no significant differences between the SITE and non-SITE groups.'[25]

2 In respect of teacher training – that the majority of the teachers felt that the training had been useful, that tv was preferable to radio and that there were significant gains in the understanding of science subjects.

3 In respect of improved agricultural practices – that 'no appreciable gains were observed,' but that tv viewing did lead to changes in behaviour.

4 In respect of health extension, nutrition and family planning – that females gained more than men in health innovations and family planning, but tv viewing 'did not increase the adoption or use of family planning methods.'

5 In respect of national integration – that 'continuous exposure to community tv viewing served to break down social barriers unthinkable earlier.'

114

The SITE project was beset with many problems. None of the stated objectives was realized fully. But non-achievement should not be attributed to the satellite as a delivery system. For the most part, non-achievement was logistical. The supporting services, both human and technological, never seemed to mesh. Despite the minuteness of the planning, and the long period of time over which preparations had been made, the project suffered from constraints which had little to do with the adequacy or inadequacy of the technology that was to be tested. The vastness of the country, the uneven quality of the administrative and other supporting services, the sheer paucity of simple maintenance facilities, the problems presented by having to produce programmes in different languages, all took their toll. Also, the experiment itself lasted only one year, hardly enough time in which even to get an experiment of such a magnitude under way. Therefore, while valuable experience was gained, one cannot conclude, on the basis of the evidence alone, that the experiment was either a success or a failure.

So we are left with little empirical evidence with which to validate the communication satellite as the catalytic development tool that technologists claim it to be. On the other hand, there is no lack of pessimism in respect of these claims, although such pessimism is not the expression either of empirical research or of rigorous theoretical thinking.[27]

A theoretical approach

In the absence of hard empirical evidence, we are compelled to fall back on theoretical thinking. We need to have both a theory of technology and a theory of development.

Arthur Clarke and several other technologists claim that technology is 'neutral': 'Like all technologies, the ability to communicate is neutral.'[28] Technologists rarely define the word 'neutral'. But if by neutral they mean that technology does not predispose those who use it, to the acceptance of values, attitudes and life styles of the societies of which they are an organized expression or product, they are going contrary to the evidence of history. We must however draw a distinction between mere 'inventions' and 'technology'. Gunpowder and the printing press were 'invented' in China and brought across to Europe where they then served to lay the foundations of European expansion and global power. But Europe did not succumb to Chinese culture by adopting their inventions! Neither did Europe absorb Arab culture by taking over the mariner's compass which was 'invented' by the Arabs. On the other hand, these 'inventions' were not organized expressions of the productive structures of medieval Chinese or Arab societies. An 'invention' is translated into 'technology' only when it is used in an organized way to extend the productive capacities of a particular society. But in order that an invention may be so translated, there must be within that society a particular conjuncture of economic, social and political circumstances which automatically guarantee its exploitation and conversion into an instrument of economic and social power. In medieval China those conditions were not available, but in Renaissance Europe they were. Similarly, the steam engine, the spinning jenny and the blast furnace did not remain as mere 'inventions' because 18th-century Britain was seething with the economic surpluses generated by the agricultural revolution of the 17th century, and the circumstances needed to convert them into engines of economic power were already in place. They then went on to transform the whole globe. It is the export and use of *such* 'inventions', i.e., technology, which have either been incorporated into the productive structures of a society, or are expressions thereof, that transmit culture.

Let us try to understand the communication satellite within this frame. Arthur Clarke may be said to have 'invented' the communication satellite in 1945. But for over a decade no one took notice of it. It was only when the rapidly expanding production machine in the advanced industrial societies began to exert pressure on existing communication systems necessitating massive investments on underground cables, etc., for instantaneous and voluminous commercial transactions, and when the whole western capitalist system came under serious threat from the rival communist system, that attention was turned to Arthur Clarke's invention. That invention has now been integrated into the production process and is to be used in turn to transform and expand it.

It is in that sense that technology is not neutral. It comes in a socio-economic-cultural-political package. By its very inner dynamic it seeks to integrate its users into the larger system of which it is the expression and the tool.

That leads us to a consideration of a theory of development. As we saw at the commencement to this paper, by the start of the 70s the development concept fashionable in the 50s and the 60s had come to be abandoned. Development had been understood to mean 'being like' the advanced industrial societies, i.e., acquisitive, affluent, consumerist and measuring progress in terms of the quantity of goods produced, possessed and consumed. Two questions are involved here. Firstly, a moral one as to whether life so lived is 'development'. But let us not delay discussing that question. Secondly, a question of economics and politics – that is to say, granted that there has been for nearly three hundred years a global economic structure that is described as the 'international division of labour' (IDL) whereby two-thirds of the world supply cheap labour and cheap raw materials to the balance third of the world, which in turn processes and manufactures and exports them back to the two-thirds at enormous profit, and granted that the one-third would never willingly yield or modify this unequal relationship, was it ever possible that the poor countries could catch up with or be like the rich countries? The development concept of the 50s and the 60s was basically contradictory in that the poor countries could never become like the rich unless the unequal relationship was restructured.

The communication theorists of the 50s and the 60s, i.e., the purveyors of the modernization theory, sought to underpin this development concept with a communication strategy. Radio and tv were to be used as substitutes for reordering economic structures, both global and domestic. It was easier to generate demand by using radio and tv, and thereby to widen the markets for the metropolitan producing countries, than to undertake painful political, social and economic restructuring. It was naively assumed that people could be motivated to learn, produce and consume by exposing them to mass media. The lack of motivation was interpreted in psychological terms as being due to a lack of psychic mobility which, it was said, could be supplied by radio and tv. The possibility that the lack of motivation could be also a product of oppressive structures and that the mere removal of such structures could be the best stimulus to production was not considered high.

The 70s were characterized by an increasingly strident demand for economic and social restructuring, both internationally and within the domestic sector. On the international plane there were demands for a 'new international division of labour' (NIDL), a 'new international development strategy' (NIDS), a 'new international economic order' (NIEO), and a 'new international information order' (NIIO). All these slogans represent demands for major global structural changes. The domestic sector has been characterized by an even greater agitation. There have been demands for land reforms, for redistribution of incomes and for greater participation and more democracy, often accompanied by insurrections, liberation struggles and even disorganized and meaningless violence often described as 'terrorism'. The international and the domestic expressions are not separate entities. They are expressions of the same reality, of an unjust and iniquitous global system. Both internationally and within the domestic sector, these strident manifestations have been met with increasing obstinacy and repression on the part of the dominant interests.

This then is the broad frame within which we have to consider the arrival of the communication satellite as the new development tool.

Relevance of the communication satellite for the Third World reconsidered

From the foregoing theoretical discussion we noted that technology is inextricably linked to a given economic base and that the global economic system is characterized by great inequalities both in respect of the distribution power within it, and in respect of access to the benefits thereof. Given such a situation, communication satellites can only result in an enormous strengthening of the power of the dominant interests and the consolidation and perpetuation of existing structures, both internationally and within domestic situations. Far from enabling 'development' as understood in the 70s and 80s, they are likely to return the global economic system to the disparities of the 50s and 60s. That is to say, contrary to claims concerning their potential for enabling interaction and participation, they are more likely to strengthen the structures of which they are the product.

Let us now re-examine the 11 claims made on behalf of communication satellites as set out earlier in this paper, within the foregoing theoretical frame.

1 National integration

One has to remember that the lack of national integration can be a manifestation of a malaise which is far more complex than is suggested by territorial vastness or the incidence of forests, mountains and deserts. Very often the lack of integration points to the need for more autonomy for the constituent national entities. Such entities have often been lumped together for colonial expediency and lack an inherent raison d'être. In such situations satellites can be used either as instruments of coercion or as a substitute for more human forms of achieving integration.

2 Administrative effectiveness

Bureaucratic concentration in the metropolis, which is largely responsible for administrative ineffectiveness in the Third World, is likely to be aggravated through a communication satellite. Officers will be able to work from the capital city, using telephones linked to the satellite, interactive radio systems, computers and other satellite-based gadgetry. But that would only give a spurious impression of efficiency whereas in fact the administrator will become less and less involved directly with the people in the villages. Eighty percent of the population of the Third World live in the villages. What administrators need most is a direct face-to-face encounter with them and not an electronic interface.

3 Delivery of education

This slogan has been used consistently, and with unerring success, to justify the introduction of tv into the Third World. Tv is recommended to the Third World not for entertainment, or for commerce, but for education! For over two decades experiments have been conducted for determining the adequacy of tv as a vehicle for education. Particular instances are American Samoa, the French Niger and SITE. But in none of these instances have we been told unequivocally that tv is the best vehicle, or even an adequate vehicle. On the contrary, there is considerable evidence to show that education is best delivered in a face-to-face interactive situation.

4 Delivery of agricultural extension

The problem of agricultural extension in Third-World countries is more than a question of access to knowledge and demonstration. It is primarily a question of land tenure, the lack of credit, exploitation by landlord and middleman, the lack of irrigation facilities, the high cost of inputs, etc. Most of these are structural and political questions. Reliance on satellites to deliver the right information presupposes that what hampers farm output and productivity is merely the lack of information. This is a grossly inadequate and naive understanding of the nature of agricultural production in poor countries.

5 Delivery of family planning

The considerations that apply to education apply here, too. Additionally, this argument presupposes that population growth is really the principal constraint on development on the Third World. It is sometimes argued that preoccupation with family planning is itself a search for an escape route out of the untidy business of undertaking structural changes. Satellites will perhaps help broaden and pave this escape route.

6 Delivery of medical and health care

The fundamental issues of medical and health care in the Third World are not related to the lack of communication but have to do with the lack of clean drinking water and the lack of protein and vitamins. They are not diagnostic but directly stemming from poverty.

7 Isolation from marketing information

This is a disability peculiar to big entrepreneurs and multinational corporations based in Third-World metropolitan centres and not a felt need among small-holding subsistence farmers and village cooperatives who constitute the bulk of the rural sector. The solution to the latter's need for fair prices is not likely to be provided by instantaneous satellite communication.

8 Region-specific cultural programming

Far from providing a stimulus to local cultures, satellites are likely to obliterate them completely. The needs of local programming and cultural renewal cannot be met by having more powerful transmission facilities but by providing appropriate software. Even existing terrestrial tv with only a single channel cannot be supplied with the software adequate for filling available air time. How much less can several channels be supplied with software? This would necessitate filling the increased channel time with alien and cheap programme material which would be disastrous for local cultures.

9 Political and social pluralism

Far from eroding the power of autocracies, satellites are likely to consolidate them beyond the capacity of even organized mass movements to challenge. Pluralism is ultimately a matter of political consciousness and not a question of technology. In the hands of centralized and autocratic governments satellites can function as powerfully as the military and the police.

10 Participation

Like pluralism, participation is a product of political consciousness, of the pressure of organized and motivated people on the structure of power. It can never be contrived, least by recourse to technological devices.

11 The capacity to cope with disasters

This again is less a matter of information than a matter of basic infrastructural and resource inadequacy. What does a community on a seacoast town in an average Third-World country do even if adequately warned of an impending cyclone? Their houses are so fragile that nothing they can do can reprieve them. And where are the people to evacuate? In what? And, once disaster has struck, satellites cannot supply resources that the society never had. In any case, advance warning is already available through existing weather satellites without Third-World countries having to have their own satellite capability.

At this point I would like to draw out what I feel lies behind the Third World's current preoccupation with communication satellites.

a) It tends to repeat the cardinal error of communication strategies of the 50s, *viz.,* the assumption that the cognitive element, i.e., access to information and knowledge, is fundamental to the development process. This may be true of certain cultures and societies, particularly of western industrial societies, where the cognitive element has been for centuries the dominant factor. The development communication paradigm of the 50s universalized this limited truth. Today, dazzled by the awesome information delivery capacity of the satellite, there is a visible return to this assumption.

b) The return to the cognitive is fundamentally an expression of an unwillingness to see the problems of Third-World poverty in structural terms. The breakdown of the development-communication paradigm at the close of the 60s saw the communication theorists of the behavioural school yield centre place to the structuralists – Schiller, Halloran, *et al.*[29] During the 70s we saw a growing tendency, particularly in Britain and Europe to perceive communication problems in structural terms. But the onset of satellite communication is doing to communication thinking what the eruption of radio and tv did to communication theory in the 50s. Apparently the hope is that this marvellous new tool will make it unnecessary to undertake the structural changes that the Third World has been agitating for.

c) The communication satellite is likely to do for the industrial-military complex in the 1980s what the steamship, the railways and the telegraph did for the colonial empires in the 1880s, but more efficiently and more irrevocably. It will help integrate the periphery to the centre in a more durable way than was possible then. Dependency will be aggravated and domination strengthened.

d) There is likely to be a willing acquiescence on the part of Third-World leaders, political and technological, to this new subservience. While the local leadership deepens its subservience to foreign interests, its strangle hold over its own rural sector will be strengthened. So there will come into existence a strong symbiotic relationship between the industrial-military complex working abroad and the domestic leadership working locally.

e) Not only will the satellite provide a strong impetus to the economic stranglehold of the industrial-military complex over the rest of the world, but it will simultaneously provide a platform for a resurgence of global cultural domination. With the arrival of direct broadcast satellites and the multi-beam high-gain satellites capable of beaming as many as 40 programmes directly into one's tv set, bypassing all terrestrial control systems, the stage is now set, at least technologically, for the obliteration of the cultures of poor societies. This will be brought about largely through the inability of poor societies to produce quality software for filling up the enormous expansion of air time that will result from placing a satellite in orbit. In the absence of local software, national networks will have no option but to buy cheap and inferior programmes from the foreign salesman who will be already at the door.

f) The goals and objectives of both the NIEO and the NIIO are likely to be severely vitiated. Both these global strategies call for major structural rearrangements. The satellite is likely to offer a technological alternative to such painful surgery.

g) At the root of this malaise is a defective understanding of the nature, causes and mechanisms of Third-World poverty. Basically, the error lies in assuming that Third-World poverty is caused primarily by lack of communication, and that its alleviation can be engineered by supplying an enormous volume of information to the widest possible community. Communication is indeed a factor in development, but the causes of poverty are mostly structural, both national and international. A massive injection of communication into an unequal structural relationship will help mostly to consolidate and deepen that inequality rather than alleviate it.

I would like to sharpen this point by using an illustration from agriculture. In the 1960s the Third World was caught up in what was described as the Green Revolution. This was basically an attempt to step up grain production in the Third World drastically, in the shortest possible time, by recourse primarily to technology – hybrid seed varieties cultured abroad. But this bequest from abroad did not come only as seed. It came in a package which included seed, artificial fertilizer, pesticides, weedicides and tractors – all of which had to be imported at increasingly high prices from the agro-business complex in the industrially advanced countries. It was in the very nature of this package that the rich farmer would benefit most from it, because of high import costs. Gross production increased sharply, as predicted, but the rich farmers grew richer and the poor, poorer. That is to say, by flowing into an unequal structural situation, technology had benefited those who were already well off and had consolidated and perpetuated the existing iniquitous power relationships in the rural sector. And few benefited as much from the Green Revolution as the agro-business complex of the advanced industrial countries!

The communication revolution in the Third World will come in a similar package. It is more likely to be a rerun of the Green Revolution scenario, except that its consequences, both beneficial (to the power managers) and deleterious (to the masses), are bound to be incomparably more far-reaching and durable.

Conclusion

Having painted this somewhat pessimistic (or optimistic – depending on one's allegiances) picture about the possible consequences of communication satellites for the Third World, I feel the need to refute some misconceptions that might arise concerning my perception of the relationship of technology to development.

While technology is never neutral, 'progress' and 'development', in whatever way we may interpret them (except in the purely spiritual), are also never possible without it! It is technology, i.e., the organized use of tools for overcoming the constraints of nature, that has propelled the human race from the earliest times. The axe and the bow and arrow were the technologies of the hunting phase. The plough enabled the human race to settle down and develop an organized community life, culture, philosophy and religion. The stirrup, the wheel and the sail gave isolated communities mobility, extended their horizons and welded them into societies and nations. Similarly – the printing press, gunpowder, the mariner's compass, the steam engine, the spinning jenny, the international combustion engine, etc., etc., down to the nuclear reactor and the silicon chip – it was technology that brought about the most fundamental changes in the way human beings related to their environment, even to the extent of eroding and transforming fundamental religious values and beliefs. No social organization or power in history has yet thwarted, for any considerable length of time, the march of technology. The Luddites tried to do it in the 18th century, but they went into oblivion and the machines they broke remained! Mahatma Gandhi and Mao Tse Tung tried to do it in the 20th century, but shortly after their deaths, the march of technology within their societies was resumed with added vigour!

And there has been no technology that has not had negative consequences. The primitive axe must have been used for killing the cave man next door as well as to fell the overhanging tree for fuel. A Roman emperor is said to have prohibited the use of water power for turning wheels used for grinding corn on the ground that it would keep the slaves idle! Motor cars cause a great deal of environmental pollution. The jet engine has resulted in the loss of thousands of lives. Every year hundreds of people die of electrocution. Similarly, the communication satellites will bring in its wake its own negative results. But in none of these instances would anyone suggest the obliteration of the technology in question because of its negative consequences.

The thrust of this paper is not that we should reject communication satellites, and much less that we should wage war against technology. I have argued that the assumptions underlying the proposal to use communication satellites in the Third World are wrong, that satellites cannot provide the solutions to problems which are primarily political, economic and sociological and that if satellites are used as an alternative to painful structural reforms, they are more likely to consolidate and perpetuate those conditions which in the first place produced the problems. In the absence of such structural reforms, both internationally and nationally (as set out in the programme for an NIEO and NIIO), satellites will most certainly benefit and strengthen the dominant interests, making the solutions even more difficult to attain.

Technology should be put at the service of *all* the human race. But in history technology has been used mostly by the dominant powers for extending and perpetuating their hegemony. A case in point is the way railway networks, telephone lines and airline traffic developed in the Third World. Indeed, communication sattelites have an important role to play, more important perhaps than the steam engine in the industrial revolution. But we must ensure that the societal, economic and political mechanisms that will guarantee that the new technology will not deepen global inequalities, are also simultaneously in place.

Whenever in history a dramatic development in technology was not matched by a corresponding rearrangement in power relationships, it ceased to be a liberating force and was transformed into an instrument of oppression. The more powerful the technology and the more pervasive its capacity for influencing individual lives and transforming the character of whole cultures and societies, the greater the need for social control and democratic accountability. We cannot afford to leave the direction and application of such technologies in the hands of entities whose social and normal accountability is constrainted by the needs of private profit. Throughout history, it has been the failure to match technological progress with social accountability that has aggravated inequalities, deepened oppression and produced enormous social violence.

References

1 Everett Klainjans, President, East-West Centre, Honolulu, from his introductory address to the Conference on Communication and Change in Developing Countries held in Honolulu in January 1975, quoted in Foreword to *Communication and Change – the Last Ten Years and the Next,* edited by Wilbur Schramm and Daniel Lerner, the University Press of Hawaii.

2 Daniel Lerner, *The Passing of Traditional Society,* 1958; Everett Rogers, *The Diffusion of Innovations,* 1963; Wilbur Schramm, *Mass Media and National Development,* 1964.

3 *Communication and Change in Developing Countries,* edited by Daniel Lerner and Wilbur Schramm, East-West Centre Press, 1965.

4 'Data on Communication Systems' in *Communication and Change in the Last Ten Years,* edited by Wilbur Schramm and Daniel Lerner, figures quoted from p 12.

5 FAO *Monthly Bulletin of Agricultural Economics and Statistics,* March 1974, p 2; UN *Yearbook of International Trade Statistics 1973.*

6 *Communication and Change – the Last Ten Years and the Next,* edited by Wilbur Schramm and Daniel Lerner, Preface to paper by economist Harry Oshima, p 15.

7 Anna Casey–Stahmer, 'Satellites for Rural Development: the Era of Experimental Satellites' in *Journal of Communication,* Vol 29 No 4 p 138.

8 Arthur Clarke, *New Communication Technologies and the Developing World,* address delivered at opening session of IPDC Council meeting, Paris, June 1981, p 14.

9 *Ibid.,* p 6.

10 *Ibid.,* p 8.

11 *Ibid.,* p 11.

12 Wilbur Schramm, 'Some Questions about Television Satellites' in *Satellite Communications and Christian Mission,* published by IMMI, Kristiansand, Norway, 1979, p 45.

13 *Peacesat Project,* Reports 1, 2 & 3, published by University of Hawaii.

14 Binod Agrawal, *Television Comes to Village – an Evaluation of SITE,* published by ISRO, Bangalore 1978.

15 Sheldon and Linda Gilberg, 'Education for Indonesia via the Palapa Satellite' in *Satellite Communications,* May 1978.

16 Ali Al-Mashat, Director General of Arabsat, 'Arabsat' in *Educational Broadcasting International,* March 1980.

17 *Uplink,* newsletter of the Rural Satellite Programme, funded by USAID, June 1981, p 5.

18 *Ibid.,* p 6.

19 John Mitchell, 'Appropriateness of Satellite Communications for the Third World' in *Media Asia,* Vol 5 No 2 p 101.

20 *Ibid.,* p 102.

21 The two best published summaries on the SITE research findings are by anthropologist Binod Agrawal of the Space Applications Centre, Ahmedabad:

Satellite Instructional Television Experiment, published by ISRO, October 1978; *SITE Social Evaluation: Results, Experiences and Implications,* published by ISRO, 1981. On pp 65–68 of the latter, Agrawal gives a list of some 28 resource publications which will be of interest to serious researchers. The *Journal of Communication,* Vol 29 No 4 also has a section devoted to summaries of some of the research findings. Bella Mody writes a competent piece, 'Lessons from the Indian Satellite Experiment' in *Educational Broadcasting International,* September 1978, pp 117–120. K E Eapen has also written fairly extensively on this subject: 'Social Impacts of Television on Indian Villages: Two Case Studies' in *Institutional Exploration in Communication Technology,* Honolulu, East-West Centre, 1978; 'The Cultural Component of SITE' in the *Journal of Communication,* Vol 29 No 4 pp 106–113. For the planning stage of SITE, see Yash Pal, 'Some Experiences in Preparing for a Satellite Television Experiment for Rural India' in *Proceedings of the Royal Society London,* 1975, pp 437–445. The most comprehensive interdisciplinary overview of the SITE proposal, written before the experiment was completed, and setting out its planning history and conceptual range, is Romesh Chander and Kiran Karuik, *Planning for Satellite Broadcasting,* UNESCO publication No 78 on Mass Communication.

22 Binod Agrawal, *SITE Social Evaluation,* summary published by ISRO, 1981.

23 *Ibid.*

24 *Ibid.*

25 Srehalata Shukla, 'Impact of SITE on Primary School Children' in *Journal of Communication,* Vol 29 No 4 p 104.

26 The inconclusiveness of the data from SITE does not seem to have deterred India's programme to develop its own domestic satellite capability. For a technological evaluation of the Indsat proposal, written before the SITE experiment was started, see Alexander Melzer, *The Social Use of India's TV Satellite,* a doctoral thesis published by the Centre for Economic Research, Swiss Federal Institute of Technology.

27 For a carping critique of the current tendency to consider communication satellites as a panacea for Third-World development problems, see Brenda Maddox, *Beyond Babel,* published by André Deutch, Chapters 6 & 7.

28 Arthur Clarke, *New Communication Technologies and the Development World,* 1981, p 10.

29 Herbert Schiller, *Mass Communication and the American Empire,* 1969; *The Mind Managers,* 1973; *Communication and Cultural Domination,* 1976. James Halloran, *Mass Media and Society,* 1974.

Advertising and the Creation of Global Markets: the Role of the New Communication Technologies

Noreene Janus
Consultant, Latin-American Institute of Transnational Studies (ILET)

Introduction

Information plays a central role in the expansion and consolidation of the transnational corporate system as a whole. In recent years the development of a broad range of highly sophisticated and efficient information technologies has provided corporate users with a qualitative advance in the fluidity of international flows of vital information. The rapid development of telematics and the creation of giant data processing, storage and retrieval networks serve the information needs of primarily military establishments and private-sector clients. These information networks have become the central nervous systems of transnational corporations, facilitating the optimization of their profits through efficient and synchronous global decision-making, timely investments, and appropriate research and development activities.

The centralized and transnational character of these global information systems has serious implications for the world political and economic order – implications which have already begun to cause serious international disputes. The major source of conflict is that access to and control over these technologies has become decisive in industrial administration and production and national economic and military strength allowing 'information-rich' countries increased power vis-à-vis the so-called 'information-poor'. Discussions of the most important international issues have emphasized that while productivity increases in some of their informatized industries enhance the competitive position of the advanced industrialized countries on the world market the information-poor face stagnating employment, productivity and growth levels and a deteriorating position in the world market. Industrial production using information technologies in advanced economies is resulting in a new international division of labour in which the traditional industries are losing comparative advantages to cheap labour. Furthermore, these countries are increasingly alarmed that the use of remote satellites and other forms of transborder flows threatens their national sovereignty. The important economic implications of the new information technologies and the international scope of the applications suggest that the issues must be analyzed within the context of larger trends in the world political and economic order such as the tendency toward the accumulation of transnational capital and the progressive weakening of state power. The principal question becomes: What role do these new information technologies play in the expansion of the transnational system as a whole and how do they help to break down barriers posed by national sovereignty?

The answers to these questions tend to stress the role of information technology in only some specific types of corporate communication: administration, sales, investments, and the monitoring of raw materials, market conditions and competitor's activities. There has been surprisingly little attention paid to the use of these new technologies for corporate marketing communications in the expansion of world consumer markets. This lack is surprising given that the survival of the transnational system depends on the perpetual creation of demand on a global scale. Recent technological advances in video systems, cable television and teletext linked to telecommunications networks (which will be referred to collectively as the 'new communication technologies' in this paper) are providing the transnational corporation with new ways to reach and expand world markets through advertising. There have been important changes in the global advertiser's ability to reach world markets, the relationship between advertising and the mass media, and, perhaps most important, the ability of sovereign states to control their own media systems. Who will control these broadcast channels has become a central issue in many international disputes about the launching of communication satellites, for example. What will the role of the advertisers be and how commercial will the system be? To understand what is at stake, and how the new communication technologies are changing the organization of advertising, one must look briefly at the two rather distinct historical periods of transnational advertising.

Historically, it may be seen that the transnationalization of US manufacturing preceded the international expansion of US marketing. The first big wave of expanding manufacturing firms, during the period from roughly 1945 to 1960, opened their overseas offices before the marketing and communication systems had been formed into coordinated international networks. These early transnationals faced serious international marketing obstacles. They generally contracted a separate local advertising agency in each foreign market where their products were produced or distributed and managed them all from their US headquarters. They suffered from a lack of control over their international image, variation in the quality of the advertising contents, accounting problems associated with multiple agency relationships, and diverse pricing, and audience/media research methods. In short, the means for implementing a coordinated international advertising strategy were unavailable at that time.[1]

Stage One: Transnationalization of advertising

During the 1960s and early 1970s, US advertising agencies set into place an extensive network of offices in Europe, Canada, Latin America, and Asia which forms the basis of transnational advertising today. During roughly the same period, television became a mass medium in nearly all the most important consumer markets of the world. Together, the formation of international networks of Madison Avenue advertising agencies and the penetration of television to the households in major consumer markets provided expanding corporations with the necessary communication infrastructure to carry out their global advertising. They were now able to achieve control over their global image, to coordinate the campaigns, to reduce costs, and to obtain centralized advertising know-how from markets all over the world.

In addition, international communication and advertising networks made the 'global campaign' possible – one standard message designed at company headquarters and transmitted to all the countries where the product is made or distributed. Since the concept of the global campaign has the appeal of increased efficiency and reduced costs, many major transnational brands and firms, including Revlon, Campbell, Marlboro, Union Carbide, Coca Cola and Esso at some period during their histories used the global campaign technique successfully. With television, these advertisers could develop their global campaigns around internationally recognized visual symbols to overcome the major obstacles posed by language diversity and illiteracy.

Atlhough the first stage of transnational advertising meant a qualitative change in the organization of global advertising, there were still significant problems facing expanding firms as they sought access to the world's consumer markets: 1) insufficient and imprecise channels of communication and feedback for advertising to specific target populations, due to the underdeveloped state of advertising know-how and communication technology; and 2) national political control over mass media systems in foreign markets limiting advertising access to broadcast channels or limiting the range of product types permitted and media time and space available. The second major stage in the history of transnational advertising – which begins with the development and use of new communication technologies – is characterized by important advances in overcoming these problems.

Stage Two: Communication technologies applied to transnational advertising

The second stage of transnational advertising is marked by the use of communication technologies to expand global markets and begins in the late 1970s and early 1980s. Although this stage is just beginning to take shape, it is clear that there will be major changes in two areas: increased accuracy in the production and distribution and feedback systems of advertising: and increased advertiser access to the broadcast systems in foreign countries. Each of these types of change will be discussed below.

Increased accuracy in the production and distribution of advertising

The new communication technologies are changing the way that advertising is being created and distributed as well as how audience and media research takes place. Perhaps most important, significant changes are taking place in the way that markets are segmented and specific sectors of the population are reached. While most of these changes have just begun to affect the way advertising is carried out inside the US, they indicate probable trends in the organization of international advertising.

1 Advertising production

Most advertising agencies rely on electronic data processing systems for such routine activities as accounting, inventory, media billing, time summaries and client profitability profiles and forecasts. Now, however, they have also begun to experiment in even what are known as the 'creative' areas. For example, computers are now being used to write some types of routine content such as real-estate advertising. The characteristics of the product are feed into the computer which selects the most important of these and turns out the finished

130

copy. These uses of communication technologies in the production of advertising are still in the experimental stages. They are, however, important indicators of future developments that will help automate other areas of advertising production and link these to electronic distribution systems.

2 Advertising distribution

In the past, national advertisers in the US have relied on slow and inefficient mechanisms to distribute their advertising campaigns nationally. They have had to edit each spot television announcement separately, and distribute them individually to the television stations in the various regional markets of the US using national mail services or private shippers. In 1979 John Blair and Co satellite distribution systems began a service which beams advertising spots to Western Union Westar I satellite.[2] These spot announcements are then picked up by earth stations in the receiving cities and taped for airing in their regular time schedules. In this way, up-to-the-minute commercial schedules are inserted in syndicated series faster and cheaper than by traditional transport systems. Furthermore, the advertiser may monitor the transmission of the spot announcements. This system, a joint project of Ogilvy and Mather advertising agency, General Foods, and Blair, provides national advertisers with distribution efficiency, instant feedback, and lower costs.[3] It will be especially useful for international advertising campaigns.

3 Media ratings and audience measures

Media ratings and audience research techniques have always been speculative and rather clumsy at best. A major problem for advertisers using the new communication technologies is that no satisfactory method has yet been developed for determining their audience ratings. Potentially, however, the new technologies offer new ratings systems with greatly increased accuracy. Interactive cable television, for example, has been used experimentally, linked to telephone lines and computers to record the media viewing behaviour of audiences in the home while another part of the system is installed in the supermarket to record the product purchases made by the viewer. In this manner, viewing patterns may, for the first time, be correlated with product purchase data. With such a system, traditional gross media ratings may become obsolete.

The significance of such computerized media and viewer ratings is that they allow the advertiser to track the individual consumer, providing the information required to produce individual or personalized advertising messages.

To complete the system, the new communication technologies also offer the means by which such personalized advertising messages may reach the well-defined specific markets that are vitally important to advertisers.

4 Market segmentation

The new communication technologies will allow advertisers greater accuracy in defining and reaching smaller, more specific segments of global markets.[4] The new video technologies – videocassettes and videodiscs – play an important role in their strategies to reach individual households or consumers with what has been called 'de-massified' or 'one-on-one' advertising. But the real breakthrough in reaching these individual markets has come through cable television. With the increased number of available channels provided by cable television, specialized programming reaches smaller, more specific audiences. This makes it economically feasible, for a tennis ball manufacturer, for example, to advertise on a tennis programme which would reach the small, limited, but highly desirable market with no waste. Advertisers may also use an entire cable channel to promote one specific product category. In the state of Massachusetts the J Walter Thompson advertising agency, one of the world's largest, is carrying out a cable 'narrow casting' experiment which involves the use of several local cable channels for advertising on an all-day basis. The viewers choose the channel according to the type of product they are interested in purchasing. Audiences are limited in size – estimated to be no more than 0.5% of the total viewing audience at any given time – but because they are those who are 'ready to buy' they are very valuable to advertisers. Both cable operators and the advertising agency are using the experiment to learn about narrow, highly targeted broadcasting and the effectiveness of longer advertising formats. The convergence of two powerful forces – more information on media and audiences and the availability of more media channels – is causing advertisers to insist that every medium be thought of as a rifle rather than as a shotgun.[5]

5 Media costs

Media costs have risen spectacularly in the US, Europe and the rapidly expanding markets of the Third World. A study of media cost increases in selected countries has shown that the print media in Saudi Arabia, for example, have increased in cost more than six times the general inflation rates for the year 1980 to 1981. In Japan television rates have increased five times the general inflation rate of the economy. And in Belgium, Spain and Finland the study found that media rate increases were 50 to 100% higher than those expected for inflation.[6] Since media costs are traditionally related to the number of people reached by the channel and the number of channels available, the new technologies with the ability to reach small, well-defined audiences through virtually unlimited channels offer substantial cost reductions to the advertisers. A 30-second advertisement on one of the approximately 50 US national cable systems costs about $500 while the three major networks charge an average of $70,000 for 30 seconds on prime-time television.

Videodiscs and videocassettes have proven very cost efficient for the production of sales catalogues of the large retail stores. To solve the problem of prohibitively high postage rates for the heavy paper-printed catalogues, Sear's, for example, has put its entire 1981 mail order catalogue on videodisc. The disc is inexpensive to produce and postage costs are minimal. General Motors is also beginning to use discs for some types of advertising.

Advertisers' access to these new communication technologies has, thus, resulted in increased efficiencies in reaching targeted segments of the market at reduced costs with instant feedback on the impact of their campaigns. This will enhance the competitive position of transnational firms producing consumer products. It will also help the advertising agencies themselves to maintain their competitive lead over local advertising agencies in each market. But the major impact of the new communication technologies on transnational expansion of consumer markets is in the increased control over broadcasting in foreign markets. Here they have proved helpful in reversing many aspects of the thirty-year-long relationship between advertisers and the media.

Increased advertiser access to broadcast media

Ultimate control over the mass media has traditionally been in the hands of the state. In privately owned systems the power of the state is expressed through legislation limiting the types and amounts of advertising allowed while in state-owned systems this control extends to include sources of financing. Access to these prized marketing channels has been the subject of constant battle as advertisers pressure for relaxation of existing legislation.

The advertisers may ultimately win the battle: the new communication technologies are significantly less regulated than traditional broadcasting.[7] This relative lack of regulation of the new technologies has important implications for the transnational expansion, both inside the US and globally.

1 Access to state-owned broadcasting

In those countries where broadcasting is still largely state-supported, advertising has been completely banned or strictly limited. Expanding corporations and their advertising agencies have engaged in long struggles to break down these barriers. Broadcasting has been a clear example of the conflict between expanding transnational capital and local states struggling to preserve their national sovereignty. The new communication technologies offer the global firms the means to circumvent existing state control over broadcasting.

Videocassettes are widely used by global advertisers, for example to penetrate Sweden where broadcast advertising is limited to a few minutes a day. The major breakthrough, however, has come with the use of satellites.

Satellite receiving areas or 'footprints' are larger than the geographical limits of most countries, making it difficult to subject satellite transmissions to the same sets of legislation that control national mass media. Diverse sets of legislation within the same receiving areas has led to various conflicts in the planned launching of several European national and regional satellites. The issue of whether to allow access by advertisers has become a major source of conflict between countries.[8] Satellites from countries allowing broadcast advertising plan to beam commercial broadcasting into countries where such types of contents are strictly limited.

Successful continent-wide advertising campaigns require that advertisers be allowed unrestricted access to broadcast systems in all receiving countries. Major agencies predict that there will be a big increase in 'multinational' campaigns once the satellites are in full operation. The success of the new 'Eurobrands' depends on access to Europe-wide advertising channels. Direct mail campaigns by satellite, for example, will be possible for all of Europe once there is an international telephone exchange available.

Over time most state-supported systems have relaxed their regulations limiting the sale of advertising. The threat of foreign-originated commercial broadcast transmissions has recently led Belgium and the Netherlands to allow more time for advertising. Although there are several ways in which national governments can still exercise their control over the airwaves (limiting the licences for purchase of Direct Broadcast Satellite receiving equipment, for example), the trend is clear: the new technologies are helping the expanding transnational system to break down remaining state control over broadcasting. As the director of international advertising of the Polaroid Corporation predicts:

To achieve maximum efficiency the local national tvs, most of which are run by the governments, will have to change somewhere along the line. They'll have to change not only the amount of commercial time but how it's presented; they'll have to change everything in order to compete against the independents and the satellites.[9]

And the chairman of Unilever, Europe's largest advertiser, predicts:

'National boundaries could, as far as television is concerned, disappear. Reception areas of the satellite might become the new marketing areas.[10]

2 Range of products and services allowed

On traditional over-the-air broadcast transmissions the trend is toward greater regulation limiting the types of products and services that may be advertised. Among the heavily restricted products are drugs and medicines, tobacco, alcohol and products directed toward children. Other restrictions cover the types of claim made, the national language used, etc. The new forms of communication technologies will not be subject to the same restrictions. A far broader range of products and services will be accepted reflecting the new trend toward 'deregulation' and the difficulties enforcing these restrictions on different forms of media. Oracle, the British ITV network's home video system, will allow the advertising of, among other products and services prohibited on traditional television broadcasting, gambling operations. This decision is justified by the fact that the teletext viewer must call up the data and therefore cannot be unwillingly exposed to the commercials. In the US, the use of cable-television systems for pornography indicates the unrestricted approach being taken with the new communication technologies.

3 Time and space available for advertising

The most troublesome limitation facing broadcast advertisers is that concerning the time available for commercials. While there are also space limitations in print media the restriction is primarily applied to broadcasting due to limited frequency space for channels. These advertising time restrictions vary according to the hour, the medium and the country.

In virtually all the new communication technologies, no time limit to advertising will be applied. Commercials of extended length have led to an entirely new concept of advertising called 'informercials'. No longer will the 30- or 60-second time-frame limit what advertisers can convey to their audiences. An entire videocassette or disc is available for commercial messages. As mentioned above, entire channels of cable television have been turned over to advertisers. Other cable channels transmitting traditional types of content – sports, movies, series, etc. – often run commercials from five to eight minutes. In a survey of advertisers using cable television as an advertising medium, it was found that one fourth of the respondents use commercials longer than the traditional 60 seconds.[11] American Express and L'Oréal are two major firms using cable television to create longer 'informercial' advertising. For the advertiser a major advantage of cable television is that the FCC does not regulate advertising time.

4 Advertiser control over media contents

At the same time as advertisers are using the new unregulated communication technologies to broadcast longer advertisements about a broader range of products and services, they are moving to take control over the general field of media contents. They have now entered the production of what are called 'advertiser-created programmes' which represents a new stage in the long relation between advertising and the mass media. Instead of limiting themselves to exerting pressure on the production process traditionally in the hands of independent production houses, networks and local stations, the advertisers now produce the contents for the new communication technologies themselves. Videocassettes, discs, and cable channels are increasingly being filled with content *entirely* produced by advertisers. The only restriction facing this form of broadcast advertising is viewer resistance.[12]

To avoid viewer rejection of these all-advertising programmes, large advertisers are beginning to create media contents which complement the products and services offered.[13] A Ford automobile dealer, for example, may prepare a videocassette or disc on travel tips and landmarks that would be offered free to customers who test-drive one of the new automobiles. Kraft Foods might similarly produce a four-volume cassette or disc providing special Christmas recipes which include the use of their food products. Or United Airlines might make a 'video brochure' about the beauty of Hawaii, its history and culture, that would also include United's fares and schedules.

Similarly, to prevent viewers from erasing or skipping over advertising messages in these 'advertiser-created programmes' programming is being developed with commercials so skillfully intertwined with other information that they cannot be removed or skipped over.[14]

5 Advertising durability

One of the factors which makes traditional broadcast advertising so expensive for advertisers is that costs are calculated on the basis of announcements which run only once. Each commercial announcement gains access to the viewer only at the time it is broadcast. The new communication technologies have begun to change the concept of advertising as a 'single-exposure' perishable item. The president of a large transnational advertising agency stressed the durable quality of videocassettes and discs using the important children's market as an example. He suggested that 'a company like Sear's – already identified commercially with Winnie the Pooh – could publish a series of videodiscs featuring Pooh characters in modern episodes. These episodes would require no intrusive Sear's commercials to identify the sponsor and they *could be enjoyed again and again like a set of children's books.'*[15]

Clearly, the coming era of communications by satellite, cable and computer will be characterized not by increased viewer control and participation in the mass media but by increased persuasion to consume. The new communication technologies will change the way the entire process of advertising is carried out. The significance of the electronic handling of production, distribution and feedback systems is that they form part of a large system that will be able to monitor individual consumers, determine their life styles and consumption habits, design personalized advertising, and then deliver it via individual channels. It must be emphasized that the versatility of the advertising process has increased significantly giving the advertiser unlimited options for contents, distribution and market size. The new communication technologies offer access to specific segments of the market from one person to an entire continent. While these developments are unfolding presently inside the United States, they have begun to shape the way that transnational advertisers view their global marketing strategies. As an advertising journal predicts,

'World commercials' may be coming in tv advertising as satellites open new markets, while elsewhere the new technologies and computers could combine to produce ad messages that would address consumers individually in the tone and manner they prefer.[16]

The implications of transnational advertising for the Third World

Third-World markets are important to transnational advertisers. The local economies are often growing faster than industrialized economies, the middle classes are expanding quickly, and markets have not yet become saturated with consumer goods. The major thrust of transnational expansion has been in the area of consumer-goods producers assembling and distributing to overseas markets. And since consumer goods traditionally require the heaviest advertising expenditures, rapid growth in consumer-goods manufacturing and distributing industries generally implies a corresponding boom in advertising expenditures. A three- to fourfold growth of total national advertising expenditures over a ten-year period is common in the Third-World countries with rapid development and heavily transnationalized economies such as Taiwan, South Korea and Singapore.[17]

However, the shift of consumption patterns toward transnational products and the creation of a new consumer culture is not always the harmonious process that the advertising industry and the manufacturers would like it to be. Local populations do not always passively accept new products which are often more expensive, of poorer quality and different from locally consumed materials and foods. There is a perpetual confrontation between transnational expansion and local cultures.[18] Product acceptance often requires that manufacturers spend large sums on advertising campaigns produced by the transnational agencies who have had decades of experience in overcoming consumer resistance.

It is still premature to assess the role that the new communication technologies will have in the transnational expansion of global consumer markets. We may use present broadcasting patterns, however, as a good indicator. The mass media in Latin-American countries, for example, tend to be more dominated by advertising than media anywhere else in the world. Empirical studies show that magazines, newspapers and television devote from 30 to 50% of their time or space to advertising.[19] Furthermore, the largest part of this media advertising is purchased by transnational firms to promote their products. In studies of Latin-American women's magazines it has been found that more than 60% of the advertising promotes transnational products while for television the figure is 80%.[20] What kinds of product do these global advertisers promote on the mass media systems of the world? Contrary to those who claim that advertising is a useful source of all types of product information, a closer look reveals that only some products are advertised: soap, pharmaceuticals and cosmetics, tobacco, processed foods and alcoholic beverages are the product groups most heavily advertised. These are also industries which tend to be dominated by transnational capital. *The same firms developing the marketing uses of the new communication technologies control the economies of many Third-World countries and dominate their mass media systems.* Given these facts, it is safe to assume that the new communication technologies, as they spread to other countries of Europe, Asia, Latin America and the Middle East, will be at the service of Kraft, Coca Cola, General Foods, Procter and Gamble, Kodak and Anderson Clayton.

These new communication technologies, while still in the initial stages of household penetration in the major consumer markets of the world, are being rapidly installed. In Latin America, several countries plan to have satellite service within the next few years. In August of 1980 Colombia announced its decision to put its own satellite into orbit. Brazil and Venezuela have also announced that they will have satellite service over their territories by 1984 or 1985. And Argentina plans an ambitious project using three satellites to cover the whole expansion of its territory.[21]

Videocassette recording technology has rapidly made its way into Latin-American markets. Sony produces video recording equipment in Brazil for export to other countries within and outside the region. A large number of households in Brazil, Venezuela and Grand Cayman Island in the Bahamas already have these products. And large areas of many countries, such as Mexico, are already wired to receive cable television.

The expansion of transnational capital, the rapid flow of marketing 'know-how' from the headquarters of Madison Avenue advertising agencies to their branch offices around the world, the importance of the perpetual creation of demand for consumer products, and the rapid installation of the new communications infrastructure suggest that the new 'information age' will also be a 'commercial age' at the global level. The way in which the advertisers plan to use the new communication technologies was clearly revealed when the magazine *Advertising World* announced a few years ago that,

> *A New York programme bounced off satellite can be 'published' as a videodisc thousands of miles away in the jungle somewhere within 24 hours and played on any home tv-set with a simple attachment.*[22]

Several important questions arise: What measures can local governments take to protect their critizens from externally orginated advertising transmitted via satellite? How can legislation keep up with developments in communication technology? How will the transnational corporations use the new technologies to circrumvent local government restrictions on the commercial content of broadcasting? The answers to these questions will influence the outcome off efforts to create a New International Information and Communication Order and to preserve national sovereignty in the face of the development of the 'Global Consumer' and the 'Global Shopping Centre'.

References

1 For a discussion of the history of the transnational expansion of US advertising agencies see N Janus, *The Making of the Global Consumer: Transnational Advertising and the Mass Media in Latin America,* unpublished PhD dissertation, Stanford University, Department of Communication. 1980.

2 *Advertising Age,* 2 April 1979, p 100.

3 Since only one print is needed for satellite transmission instead of multiple prints sent by mail to each market, the advertiser may reduce costs considerably. Paramount pictures is reported to save $500,000 annually with satellite advertising distribution systems (*El Nacional,* Mexico, 22 August 1981, p 11).

4 The apparent contradiction between the search for global-sized markets and for small localized or individualized markets is discussed in recent theoretical work about the stages of the transnationalization of capital. R Trajtenberg and R Vigorito in *Economía y Política en la Fase Transnacional: Algunas Interrogantes* (Mexico: ILET, 1982) describe transnationalization as a historical process with an early and a mature stage. While the mature stage may be characterized by increased rationalization of global production and consumption, the early stage, which includes the present, is characterized by a multiplicity of local markets and a great diversity of production processes developed simultaneously in the various local world markets. These two sizes of market – global and local – are not contradictory but rather complementary and exist side by side during the early stages of transnationalization.

5 Editorial, *Advertising Age,* 13 October 1980.

6 M Hook, 'Media Inflation' in *Advertising World,* July 1981, p 26.

7 In the US there are few restrictions limiting advertiser access to the new communication technologies which reflects in part technological considerations which make regulation more difficult to implement. This attitude must be understood, however, as a part of the larger trend toward media deregulation.

8 This conflict over the nature of European satellites is described in G Fauconnier, *The 'Enfant Terrible' in European Satellite Projects: Lux-Sat* and H J Kleinsteuber, *Direct Broadcasting Satellite (DBS) – Policy of the Federal Republic of Germany.* Both papers presented to the Tenth Annual Telecommunications Policy and Research Conference, Annapolis, Maryland, April 1982.

9 B K Garson, 'Polaroid Aims High for Mass Reach in Europe' in *Advertising World,* January 1981, p 7.

10 D Chase, 'Orr: National Boundaries Could, as Far as Television is Concerned, Disappear' in *Advertising Age,*[20] October 1980, p 4.

11 'Survey Finds Cable Still Has Doubters' in *Advertising Age,* November 1981, p 66.

12 Some advertising agencies feel that the fact that viewers can skip over or erase advertising on the new technologies will encourage the creation of more appealing and more informative advertising as a means to avoid viewer rejection.

13 The creation of media contents that complement the commercial messages they contain is not new; what is new is that the production of these complementary media

contents is increasingly in the hands of the advertisers themselves rather than production houses or networks.

14 Keith Reinhard, president of Needham, Harper and Steers advertising agency quoted in 'New Media Programming View: "Video Publishing" ', in *Advertising Age,* 24 November 1980, p 68.

15 *Ibid.*

16 *Advertising Age,* 20 October 1980, p 2.

17 N Janus, *op.cit.*

18 N Janus, 'Advertising and the Mass Media: Transnational Link Between Production and Consumption' in *Media, Culture and Society,* Vol 1981 N°3, pp 13–23.

19 *Ibid.*

20 *Ibid.*

21 H Schmucler and Armand Mattelart, *América Latina en la Encrucijada Telemática,* ILET, Mexico, 1982.

22 *Advertising World,* October 1978, p 20.

INFORMATION AND SOCIETY SERIES

The impact of computer technology on society is growing rapidly. The need for understanding and debate is enormous. This new series, coordinated by Transnational Data Reporting Service, Inc (TDRS), is one essential step. The series is edited by Jan Freese, chairman of the Swedish Data Inspection Board and an internationally well-known expert on the question of computers and society, and G. Russell Pipe, editorial director, TDRS.

Becker, Jörg, editor
Information Technology and a New International Order

Information technology, which has resulted in Telematics and Transborder Data Flows is quickly becoming part of the North-South dialogue – or conflict. Many of the political, social-cultural and economic aspects of this issue are presented in the book.

Hamelink, Cees J
Transnational Data Flows in the Information Age

This study is about the most potent form of telecommunication: transnational data flows. It sets out to describe the main actors and their impact on society. The context of the analysis is the information age: the recognition that information is becoming the most operative factor of society.

Freese, Jan
Vulnerability or Robustness in the Computerized Society

Modern technological, import and export depending society was already before computerisation very vulnerable. The new technology has made the margins still more narrow. The book presents how to make society robust again.

Freese, Jan – Pipe, Russel
Privacy Laws and Computerized Information

More and more countries legislate in the field of privacy and computers. The book presents the different privacy laws as well as the result of national cooperation in OECD and the Council of Europe.